Roman Empire

The Ancient World Economy & the Empires of Parthia

(The History From the Founding of Ancient Rome to the Fall of the Roman Empire)

Arnoldo Mason

Published By **Gautam Kumar**

Arnoldo Mason

Roman Empire: The Ancient World Economy & the Empires of Parthia (The History From the Founding of Ancient Rome to the Fall of the Roman Empire)

ISBN   978-1-9994163-4-8

Legal & Disclaimer

The information contained in this book is not designed to replace or take the place of any form of medicine or professional medical advice. The information in this book has been provided for educational & entertainment purposes only.

The information contained in this book has been compiled from sources deemed reliable, and it is accurate to the best of the Author's knowledge; however, the Author cannot guarantee its accuracy and validity and cannot be held liable for any errors or omissions. Changes are periodically made to this book. You must consult your doctor or get professional medical advice before using any of the suggested remedies, techniques, or information in this book.

Table Of Contents

Chapter 1: Prehistory Roman-Italy Background

Italy has generally been a numerous state, with neighborhood variety formed with the aid of the usage of the fall apart of the Roman Empire and its persisted life to nowadays. Prior to the Roman invasion, Italy end up a numerous series of peoples, languages, and civilizations. However, our knowledge of these pre-Roman communities is limited, and a whole reconstruction in their historical history from prehistoric times is not feasible. Archaeology is the sole direct proof for the time earlier than Rome's development, and it serves as the foundation for comprehending Italy at the begin of records.

The shift from the Bronze Age (2d millennium BC) to the Iron Age (early first millennium BC) is appeared with the beneficial resource of archaeologists as a watershed moment in early Italian cultural facts. The nature of this shift and whether or no longer or no longer there has been continuity many of the 2 or a cultural 'break up' are hotly discussed topics. The maximum hard problem is describing the Late Bronze Age's transitional length (approximately 1200-900 BC). However, the cloth manner of existence of Italy inside the Bronze Age in advance than spherical 1200 BC diverged dramatically from the iron-age civilizations that arose inside the 9th century.

The maximum tremendous feature of bronze-age Italy is its cultural cohesion, which contrasts dramatically with the nearby version of succeeding intervals. This homogeneity is visible in the duration's function pottery, a kind of notably polished clay with etched geometric patterns found at some point of the peninsula in net internet websites loads of kilometers aside, but with little or no discernible version in bureaucracy or decorative troubles. Other artifacts, like bronze gadget and guns, have a similar uniformity.

The net web sites are spread throughout the peninsula, however a shocking quantity of them are centered within the hilly center place. Archaeologists have advanced the decision 'Apennine lifestyle' to explain the Italian Bronze Age civilization. The Apennine civilization existed from more or much less 1800 to 1200 BC. Although maximum of the cloth is the surrender end end result of chance finding instead of deliberate excavation, it is low priced to infer that the populace changed into quite small. Much of the land place become included in wooded place or forest, and settlements were modest; not some thing extra than a small hamlet has but been decided. The number one monetary device grow to be based definitely, at the least in element, on transhumant pastoralism, a type of stock-elevating in which flocks are moved to highland pastures inside the early summer time and however to the lowlands inside the fall.

The archeological record shows widespread modifications in the overdue Bronze Age, beginning about 1200 BC. These consequences may be examined below 3 sections.

1. There is a big rise within the variety of net sites and the style of artifacts represented in every. These sports very manifestly propose an boom in population; there may be moreover robust proof of agreement growth. This population boom maintains at some stage within the Iron Age.

2. Funerary customs are changing, with cremation replacing inhumation in masses of areas of Italy. The new burial approach is as an alternative extremely good. The creation of cremation in peninsular Italy end up positioned with the resource of recent sorts of pottery, because the Apennine way of life become in the long run changed with

the aid of the use of a modern-day day lifestyle called 'Protovillanovan'v'P.

3. Toward the perception of the Bronze Age, good sized cultural versions in the course of regions of Italy emerged. The set up order of appreciably great nearby cultures in Italy changed into nicely underway with the aid of the begin of the Iron Age, which maximum researchers in recent times date to about 900 BCE.

COPPER AND BRONZE AGE

Under the effect of 'warrior' immigrants from number one Europe, Italy began out to go into the Copper Age. There are three essential centers: Remedello in Brescia within the north, Polada from a hamlet on Lake Garda in the south, and Rinaldone in Tuscany and Gaudo near Paestum on the Italian peninsula. The earller Neolithic people survived in detail because of the modern-day influences, but the new steel come to be too uncommon to replace stone for the majority of each day equipment and implements.

Bronze Age Italy end up divided into specific cultural areas: one within the north and one alongside the Apennines. In the north, ordinary development came about across the Lakes and inside the Po valley from Neolithic instances onwards, but within the middle or later Bronze Age, a contemporary segment emerged with settlements named Terremare after the 'black earth' (terra mara), which modern farmers use as a fertilizer because of its excessive nitrogen content material material fabric. These cities have been supposed to be of a ordinary layout, with huts built on wooden systems on pile foundations and separated into blocks via parallel roadways.

The Terramaricoli were no longer Roman forebears; they will be considered 'cousins' of the Palafitticoli of the Lakes, however they had been most in all likelihood latest immigrants from the middle Danube location. They had been mainly agriculturalists and livestock producers, at the identical time as many persevered to are seeking boars, deer, bears, and perhaps fish. Fowl and geese entered the farmyard, while horses had been often achieved for drought. Their cities encompass stays of flax, beans, lentils, two forms of wheat, and wild stop result which include hazelnuts, pears, and apples. They labored with wood, bone, and horn, in addition to steel, and that they continued to manufacture textiles and ceramics. Their pottery become particular, however severa.

Their cremation cemetery and the truth that they spoke Indo-European had been critical features in their civilization. As they maintained touch with the Danube place, they created a communique conduit thru which the extra northern Bronze Age civilization increased southward, organising an important link in Europe's exchange networks. They were each makers and importers, and their gadgets in the long run made their way south into metallic-bad Apennine Italy.

The Apennine civilization peaked about 1500 BC and was notably plenty a great deal less developed than northern corporations, regardless of the fact that being more critical to peninsular Italy. The human beings were descendants of the Neolithic and Copper Age populations, jumbled collectively with some 'warriors' who can also moreover have arrived in small companies from out of doors (from the Aegean worldwide) and landed in Apulia or on the west coast. Their semi-nomadic way of lifestyles may want to have aided in the unfold of their language, that could have been an ancestor of the Samnites' later Umbro-Sabellian dialect.

Their darkish burnished pottery, which come to be each handsome and numerous in format, has been observed for the duration of Italy, at the side of the destiny website of Rome, south-east Emilia, Etruria, Latium, Campania, Apulia, and Lipari. Some researchers accept as genuine with that this civilization modified into the vital detail figuring out impact in the makeup of the Italic human beings from Lipari to the Po.

In the past due Bronze Age, the Terramaricoli and Apennine clans began out to converge, in all likelihood seeking out copper from Etruria. By the 11th century, a few Apennine population had established themselves in open companies along the Adriatic and the Po's mouth. The northerners labored the metallic and started out out transport it to Etruria and alongside the Adriatic coast as far south as Tarentum, in which an Apennine town had traded with the Mycenaeans earlier than their empire fell.

From about 1150 BC, a extra regular civilization superior over Italy, and the 2 important tribes came nearer collectively.

Cremation and urn fields first arose approximately a thousand BC in severa locations in which inhumation had previously ruled, but the historic Apennine civilization and inhumation lasted a ways into the Iron Age.

The degree to which enterprise adventurers sailed out into western seas from Minoan Crete is unknown, notwithstanding the fact that a few have left their mark on Sicily and Lipari. The Mycenaean Greeks answered more forcefully, with their presence in Sicily and Lipari recorded in advance than 1400 BC. They extended their alternate from the heel of Italy up the Adriatic coast to Sicily and Lipari. Mycenaean pottery has been determined at Syracuse, Mylae in northeast Sicily, Lipari, the island of Ischia near Naples, and 5 pieces relationship lower again to greater or an awful lot less 1250 BC in Luni in Etruria.

Lipari and the adjacent volcanic Aeolian Islands, located about 25 miles northeast of

Sicily, owe their early importance to the nearby obsidian, which emerge as mined already in Neolithic instances. Greek pottery added in the path of the Bronze Age has served as vital dating cloth. The Middle Bronze Age companies on Lipari's fortress and one-of-a-type islands had been destroyed approximately 1250 BC, and were modified via an Apennine organization civilization. This new cultural section (Ausonian II) need to have started out with new invaders from the peninsula and lasted at least till the 9th century. Ausonian civilization gave manner to the Early Iron Age and the Villanovans, whilst Lipari material is analogous with early Bronze Age relics from Rome's Palatine and Forum.

ITALIAN IRON AGE

The human beings of Italy at some level within the Iron Age had been split into organizations: individuals who practiced cremation and people who practiced inhumation. Early iron-age cremation cultures are essentially placed in northern Italy and lowland regions along the Tyrrhenian coast, together with Etruria, Latium, and Campania. The majority of the peninsula become populated by inhuming civilizations, apart from a cemetery at Fermo in Picenum that blanketed Villanovan cremation burials.

Northern Italy has numerous precise iron-age civilizations. One of them is represented thru a hard and fast of exquisite cremation cemeteries in the lake basin of Lombardy and Piedmont, referred to as the 'Golasecca subculture'. This civilization, which existed from the ninth to the fourth century BC, is regularly referred to as the 'Este tradition'. From the 9th to the 1/three century BC, the Este (or Ateste) civilization thrived inside the northeastern part of the Po easy. Its primary websites include cremation cemeteries at Padua, Vicenza, Oppeano Veronese, and Este (ancient Ateste).

The Situla humans of the Este life-style had near interplay with northern Italy's 0.33 and most large iron-age civilization, called the Villanovan life-style. This civilization emerged north the Apennines in Emilia-Romagna and is known as for the area near Bologna wherein it end up within the beginning determined in 1853. Bologna itself became a distinguished iron-age city that preserved its Villanovan identification from its inception about 900 BC till it modified into conquered with the resource of the Etruscans at the surrender of the 6th century.

The majority of the evidence comes from funeral settings, and the best distinguishing issue of Villanovan society is the burial rite itself. The ashes have been deposited in a biconical urn and sealed with a lid, which have become frequently an inverted bowl but also can be formed like a helmet. The urn become then inserted proper into a deep hole (pozzo) and included with a stone slab. Latium has a peculiar nearby variety, with 'hut-urns' or ossuaries within the guise of about designed residing-homes. This geographical variety, lengthy labeled as "southern Villanovan," is now regularly called the "Latial way of existence" (cultura laziale).

In Etruria and Emilia-Romagna, the Villanovan civilization stands out from the previous time. Although there are obvious similarities in burial practices and grave furnishings among Villanovan and Protovillanovan, the region and distribution of agreement websites are extraordinarily distinct.

The inhuming civilizations of peninsular Italy may be categorized into 3 education: the fossa-cultures of Campania and Calabria, which have been influenced via Greek colonies, the Apulian tradition, and the Picene way of life. During the Iron Age, those civilizations advanced one after the opportunity and have been impacted via interactions with Illyrian peoples across the Adriatic. Both Apulia and Umbria-Picenum were poorly recorded at some stage in the early Iron Age, but they in the end installation particular material civilizations and maintained self retaining customs. The Apulian civilization is diagnosed for its geometric ceramics, this is particular to Apulia in Italy. The civilizations of Umbria and Picenum are a lot much less resultseasily defined, although they'll be represented through extraordinary artifacts, together with stone burial stelae from Novilara (Pesaro) and a life-period warrior discern from Capestrano. Fragments of comparable sculptures were determined at severa Picenum net net websites, the most high-quality being the helmeted head from Numana (Ancona). These civilizations have been without a doubt warrior societies, as indicated by using manner of the use of the gadget positioned of their burials.

ORIGIN OF ITALIAN LANGUAGE

Latin has impacted numerous languages in the route of Europe and the Western worldwide. It replaced Greek and Aramaic due to the truth the Empire's language and ultimately have grow to be the first rate language of the Catholic Church at a few degree inside the Middle Ages.

During a critical duration in Europe's boom, Latin have emerge as the dominant lingua franca, irrespective of Greek being the intellectual language of the East.

Throughout the Renaissance and Baroque centuries, the Roman language have become the primary method of communique for intellectuals, notably influencing the development of technological knowledge and treatment.

Copernicus, as an example, wrote his main works completely in Latin, and the phrases used to establish the sciences are despite the fact that used nowadays.

Latin had a extensive impact on the formation of Romance and Germanic languages. The language I'm writing in, considered the lingua franca of the modern-day global, is primarily derived from Latin and shares syntax with Romance languages like French. Every phrase we are pronouncing perpetuates the way of existence of Rome.

We moreover use the Roman script in our written phrases. The Latin script is a totally specific aggregate of numerous traditions from the Empire, originating from an Etruscan version of Greek writing. It is taken into consideration the maximum 'Roman' of the Empire's legacy. Languages are frequently categorised as Indo-European or not.

Indo-European (IE) refers to languages spoken in Europe and factors of Western and Southern Asia that percentage vocabulary, grammar, and morphology and are idea to have originated from a not unusual inventory for the reason that 19th century. However, it's miles dubious if a single IE language existed at a particular time and region. The IE own family is prepared into cautiously associated language businesses, now not like unique households along with Germanic, Slavic, and Iranian. Scholars frequently use the metaphor of an IE own family tree, with numerous groupings or sub-families springing from the imperative stem. Italy's languages include a unique magnificence referred to as 'Italic'.

Latin, spoken entirely in Latium to the south and east of the Tiber valley, is one of the Italic languages. Dialectal variances exist among Latin spoken at Rome and special Latin settlements. The Faliscans, who resided on the proper monetary group of the Tiber north of Veii, can also constitute one such dialect. A newly discovered inscription indicates that a number of the morphological developments of Faliscan had been moreover gift in the language spoken in Satricum, a Latin hamlet placed 80 kilometers south. This suggests that 'Faliscan' is exceptional a dialect of Latin.Venetie, a language spoken in northeastern Italy, and likely the language of the Sicels, a nearby people of jap Sicily, are closely related to Latin (and likely Faliscan, if it is a separate language). However, the 'Sicel' language isn't always well documented. Scholars communicate over with the ones languages as 'West Italic'. The Italic languages had been historically dispersed throughout important, eastern, and southern Italy and are carefully associated. It consisted of important elements: Umbrian, as evidenced with the aid of inscriptions from Umbrian towns, and Oscan, spoken by using manner of the southern Apennines, Samnites, Lucanians, and Bruttians, in addition to the bulk of Campanian residents. The precious Apennine location (the Abruzzi district) is concept to have spoken Oscan or Oscan-type dialects, such as the Sabines, Marsi, Paeligni, Marrucini, Vestini, and Picenes, in addition to the Aequi and Volsci, although documentary evidence is constrained or non-existent.

Italy's IE languages don't have any similarities with exclusive Italic languages Greek, spoken in Greek colonies in southern Italy due to the fact the eighth century, Celtic, spoken inside the Po valley and along the Adriatic coast from Ravenna to Rimini, and Messapic, spoken in Italy's 'heel'.

Chapter 2: Origin of Rome

Archaeological Evidence

The first businesses in Old Latium seemed on low hills or spurs that achieve from the relevant Apennines to the coastal plain. Rome, located in a fortified place with a sufficient deliver of glowing water and clean get right of entry to to the sea, dominated the primary herbal routes of communique in crucial Italy. These routes included the Via Salaria (the 'Salt Road') and the coastal road from Etruria to Campania. The Forum Boarium has remnants of Apennine pottery from the middle Bronze Age, that are a number of the oldest signs and symptoms of human hobby within the place.

The earliest signs of eternal house at the internet site of Rome date lower back to type of 1000 BCE, with a handful of cremation tombs within the Forum. Similar tombs were placed inside the Alban Hills, Pratica di Mare (Lavinium), and possibly Ficana, in addition to in the Sabine region at

Palombara Sabina and Campo Reatino. This fabric represents the popularity quo of a separate archaeological facies in Old Latium, called the 'Latial way of lifestyles' (cultura laziale).

The initial phase of the Latial way of life, which lasted from approximately one thousand to 900 BCE, came about during the last level of the Italian Bronze Age, and the Latial material is a nearby version of the Protovillanovan civilization. In its early tiers, the Latial civilization is recorded really through tombs, with the burial ritual being its most distinguishing characteristic. The maximum critical detail is the hut-urn, a receptacle for ashes that resembles a hint residing-house.

There is little appeared approximately the community to whom the ones first cremations belonged, and no settlements from the primary Latial period have not all commenced been determined. However, considerably more potent evidence exists for the second phase, which marks the begin of the Iron Age in Latium. There isn't any damage in continuity from the preceding period, however the amount of content material material grows extensively, and masses of latest websites rise up inside the meantime.

The findings of this observe have significantly altered our information of the Iron Age in Latium, which is now higher documented than some different place of Italy. The Osteria dell'Osa, a cemetery at the banks of Lake Castiglione, is the most sizeable early Iron Age net page, with loads of graves unearthed methodically the use of current techniques.

The Osteria dell'Osa cemetery preserves funerary proof from the early half of of the second Latial phase (IIA, c. 900-830 Be), whilst cremation and inhumation had been practiced simultaneously. The ritual of cremation became reserved absolutely for men, no matter the reality that best for a choose out organization, thinking about that inhumation tombs comprised each genders. The technique required full-size exertions and cash in view that burning a body have become tough, and the small artifacts interred with the ashes might have needed to be carefully created for the occasion.

The grave furniture (corredo) have become made of miniature earthenware and bronzes that created a well-defined symbolic totality. The everyday corredo consists of 3 or four food and drink garage containers, similarly to cups, bowls, and plates. The bronzes encompass a brooch, a razor, and tiny weapons, normally a spear and once in a while a sword. The symbolic reason of this set of artifacts is plain: it represents the deceased person's transition from one existence to some other, providing him with the equipment he wishes for each day residing and the fulfillment of his social responsibilities inside the network.

There is likewise proof of greater unique makes use of, collectively with graves containing statuettes of human beings making services, a small bronze sacrificial knife, a ritually shattered vase, and a few tiny pots. Another tomb is top notch in that the entire corredo is housed in a huge square hut-urn in location of the same old dolium, indicating a far massive shape of dwelling-house.

Inhumations had been simpler, with the deceased being buried complete length in square trench graves. Males were frequently followed via or three pots (fashionable period) and a brooch, however no weapons. Women were buried with some vases, personal decorations which encompass brooches, earrings, glass and amber beads, and a spindle whorl. A constrained amount of lady tombs embody more precisely crafted earthenware and masses of private decorations, including spindle whorls, bobbins, loom weights, and distinctive weaving-associated artifacts.

Cremation appears to have ceased truly via manner of the give up of this era, and section IIB is represented handiest thru inhumations. This suggests that a specific funeral ceremony became nevertheless precise for men of recognition within the society, even though it has left no trace in archeological records.

Early Settlements

The funerary evidence indicates a number one social organisation, with corporations divided thru way of kinship and people categorized with the aid of age, gender, and practical responsibilities in the circle of relatives and community. There is little indication of economically superb education or lasting social stratification. The proof elements to a subsistence financial device centered on the production of primitive grains and legumes, complemented through cattle husbandry.

Grain kinds determined in botanical remains within the Roman Forum embody einkorn wheat (10%), emmer wheat and/or spelt (fifty eight%), barley (32%), lentils (Vicia faba), and peas (Pisum). Animal bones from graves in Rome and a few place else display a desire for pigs over livestock and 'caprovines' (sheep and goats). Many graves have spindle whorls and loom weights, suggesting that wool have become produced.

A thorough exam of the sustenance financial machine of early Latin corporations necessitates a controlled clinical research of plant and animal stays from home settings in habitation web web sites. Pottery grow to be essential, hand-made 'impasto' that each own family created for its very private home cause. The presence of spindle whorls in truely all female burials suggests home textile manufacture. The sole specialized competencies become metalworking, which emerge as maximum in all likelihood finished through domestically based without a doubt artisans who controlled required trade with metallic-generating areas, specially Etruria and Calabria.

During the early days of the Roman Empire, communities had been tiny settlements with an expected populace of one hundred people. However, in the end of phase IIB, the settlement pattern shifted as settlements commenced out to merge and shape bigger nucleated devices. For instance, near Lake Castiglione, a great united community commenced to increase at the website on line of the eventual city of Gabii, on the identical time as in Rome, the habitation place become improved from the Palatine to cowl the Capitol and Forum. Surface research determined out comparable clusters of tiny village websites at Ardea and Lavinium, and is the reason the dispersed agencies of graves within the Alban Hills.

During phase IIB, the populace of Old Latium grew, with older web sites developing in duration and severa new net web web sites rising. Surface surveys and accidental findings moreover display that numerous excavated internet web sites within the area's north and east had been interested about the useful resource of the give up of the 9th century. However, there may be no indication of equivalent population increase in the Alban Hills region. A new quick evaluation of change routes and communications in Old Latium concludes that the Alban Hills place is in decline, whilst other web sites on the apparent are getting extra vital.

The late Bronze Age and the past due 9th and eighth centuries provide two extremely good models for the area. The former depicts the Alban Hills due to the fact the hub of a communications community that links southern Etruria, coastal Latium, and every indoors and coastal routes to Campania. Rome has become the nodal element of routes from Etruria to the south, with the emergence of recent settlements together with La Rustica, Laurentina, and Decima, as well as the eclipse of the Alban Hills.

The new agreement patterns did not bring about rapid changes to the social corporation of the settlements, which is probably categorised as 'proto-city' in area of city. Settlements remained to be made from primary wattle-and-daub cottages with thatched roofs supported with the useful resource of wooden helps. These cottages have a undying appeal and may be made in a couple of hours using with ease accessible substances, requiring no expert information.

Foundation Of Rome: The Legends (Romulus and Remus)

Legends concerning the founding of Rome, and versions on them, abound in Greek and Roman literature. According to popular notion, while King Latinus reigned over the Laurentian aborigines, some Trojans commanded by means of using Aeneas came after their city was destroyed. Aeneas married Lavinia, Latinus' daughter, and at the same time as the King died, he reigned over the Trojans and aborigines, who had been now referred to as Latins. After constructing the city of Lavinium, Aeneas died and have become modified by using the usage of his son Ascanius, seemed to the Romans as Iulus, who installation Alba Longa. After twelve kings dominated in Alba, a prince named Amulius unlawfully took the throne in lieu of his older brother Numitor, who had forced his daughter, Rhea Silvia, to end up a Vestal Virgin.

The twins Romulus and Remus were miraculously spared from drowning and washed up below a fig tree referred to as

Ruminalis near the Palatine. They slew Amulius, established Numitor, and went off to set up a metropolis in the vicinity wherein they were rescued. However, whilst Romulus preferred to construct on the Palatine, Remus decided on the Aventine. The omens subsidized Romulus' preference, however in defiance, Remus vaulted over his brother's developing wall and modified into killed via way of manner of him.

This delusion have become created with the aid of manner of mixing traditions: Roman recollections that ascribed Rome's foundation to Romulus and Greek versions in which Aeneas changed into the principle function. Greek poets constantly created tales about the exploits of severa heroes, drastically Odysseus, who mounted towns following the destruction of Troy. The myth of Aeneas' journey from Troy reached Etruria by using the use of the 6th century, and as a minimum seventeen vase artwork represent the incident. Votive statuettes depicting Aeneas sporting his father Anchises in break out from Troy determined at Veii have been dated to the sixth century, despite the truth that other experts suppose they will be no older than the destruction of Veii on the start of the fourth century.

Variations at the number one reminiscences flourished, with amongst 25 and thirty separate versions attributed to Greek authors, all of which differed from the following expert Roman narrative. These repercussions can not be explored massive, but the legends of Romulus and Remus, in addition to Aeneas, must be considered for the reason that each had a large impact on later Roman feeling.

The mythology of Romulus and Remus, a important issue of Rome's narrative, has been studied in some of strategies. Some revel in it's far an historic nearby tale, at the same time as others count on it's miles a late literary fabrication. It had in reality advanced with the resource of using the give up of the fourth century, thinking about the fact that early Roman cash depicted the she-wolf with twins. However, it's far fantastic that the an entire lot older Capitoline wolf monument (c. 500 BC) changed into related to Romulus and Remus; the twins' statues had been brought after the Renaissance.

The twins' names have generated confusion, for the cause that Romans stated them as Romulus and Remus, on the identical time as Greek authors used Romulus and Romus. One university of perception holds that the Greeks fabricated Romus as the eponymous founder of Rome, and that when the Romans, who named their founder Romulus, heard about Romus, they united the two as twins, converting the call Romus to Remus. A extra complex model claims that Romulus emerge as truely the Latin form of the Greek Romus, and that the later Greeks, ignorant of this, assumed they needed to deal with two men and women and consequently superior the twins. When this model reached Rome, the Romans followed it with the sole trade being Romus to Remus.

It isn't unreasonable to do not forget an historic Roman beginning location, for the purpose that every nouns are real Roman names. Archaeological proof well-known that cities merged at an early period in Rome's statistics, and the myth also can have originated from the presence of early village heads.

Only some Greek authors and no Roman writers, other than Sallust, considered Aeneas the inspiration of Rome. The Romans may moreover have based totally their Trojan lineage on Aeneas, the Latins' progenitor in preference to the builder in their metropolis. His fable can also have reached Rome thru southern Etruria and Veii, in which he changed into well-known as a minimum within the fourth or sixth century, as verified via manner of the use of the statuettes.

There have been moreover differing evaluations approximately the exact date of the town's founding. Ennius, a poet, appears to have lengthy beyond again past Timaeus' date of 814 BC to about 900, however Fabius Pictor and Cincius Alimentus pushed it to 748 and 728, respectively. Later, beneath Augustus, the reminiscences had been given their maximum literary reputation in Livy's History and Virgil's Aeneid.

Story of The Early Roman Kings

Skepticism about the existence of kings in early Rome is unjustified. The presence of Indo-European peoples is proven thru their political evolution, the interregnum, the life of the rex sacrorum and Regia, and the time period regei on an inscription located inside the Forum underneath the Lapis Niger near Romulus' grave. There changed into no kings' faith, and there may be no indication of divine starting vicinity in their names or narratives, therefore rejecting them as gods is incorrect. The concept that the seven kings signify the seven hills has likewise proved fruitless. However, maximum of Roman facts about them is incorrect, and their non-public existence is uncertain. The monarchs that succeeded Romulus were Titus Tatius, Numa Pompilius, Tullus Hostilius, Ancus Marcius, Tarquinius Priscus, Servius Tullius, and Tarquinius Superbus. The canonical listing modified into compiled inside the fifth century. The names of these heroes range from the ones of the famous guys of the duration, indicating that they were not made as an awful lot as link succeeding heroes to the kings of vintage. Their gentile names appeared later in Republican information. Although each king ought to have had a protracted reign between the muse of Rome and the Republic (753-510), it's miles feasible that they have been Rome's remaining seven rulers. In assessment to village management, Rome's monarchy is going again to the Seventh Century, whilst the Four Regions have been mounted. The palace's (Regia) strategic placement at the foot of the Velia lends assist to this.Nine

Romulus and Titus Tatius have to be seemed as legendary characters. Romulus is stated to have expanded his populace in strategies: through developing a criminal steady haven on the Capitol and plotting the fabled rape of Sabine women. By organizing a celebration in honor of Consus, the god of the granary or garage, he attracted numerous Sabines and different pals to Rome. However, his troops stole the women for him. Titus Tatius, King of Cures, led the Sabines in the direction of Rome, taking pictures the Capitol through Tarpeia's treachery. Tarpeia betrayed the citadel, handiest to collect the crushing weight of their shields rather than the promised gold armlets. Following the war, Sabine girls interfered to restore peace and reconciliation most of the Romans and Sabines, with Romulus ruling at the Palatine and Tatius on the Capitoline. Until Tatius' loss of life, the two kings met with elders and those in the valley of the Forum, wherein they'd fought. After Tatius died, Romulus dominated by myself until Mars carried him to heaven on a chariot.

These legends have little ancient fact, but they decorate severa issues.

Romulus and Tatius' dual monarchy might also provide mild at the beginnings of the Roman Republic's collegiate magistracy. The fable of the asylum, which became a proper in Greek organizations, could have been created to represent Rome's destiny generosity in developing citizenship, or to provide an reason for the start location of a 'holy' position atop the Capitol, which embody a lightning strike internet internet web page. Historians may moreover dismiss the rape of Sabine ladies as an try and offer an cause in the back of Roman marriage requirements, among unique reasons. Some contend that the narrative of a Sabine colony on Rome's hills and its union with a Palatine town, similarly to the related legends, have to be really overlooked. Rome had an early Sabine have an impact on, as proven by way of using the mixing of Sabine terminology into their language and the advent of Sabine deities in valid rites. The Romans associated the mysterious Quirinus with both Mars and the deified Romulus. The call may additionally take a look at to the Quirinals or Quirites, due to the truth the Romans used to call themselves.

Archaeological evidence famous that the early populace of the Quirinal and Esquiline resembled the Roman Sabines. Tatius might be a latinized version of a Sabine call in desire to an Etruscan call. However, he's a shadowy man or woman within the narrative, and his call is defined on the subject of the 'Romulean' tribe Tities and the priesthood of sodales Titii. However, his legend may additionally replicate a big historical truth.10

The following 3 kings are represented as sturdy priests, warriors, and regulation-givers, but are they actually guys? Although many establishments and behaviors were wrongfully associated with the ones heroic personalities, contemporary-day critics have stripped them in their trappings, allowing the opportunity that they have been actual humans.

Numa Pompilius, a Sabine, is said to have settled on the Quirinal. The name Numa can be Etruscan, but Pompilius is Sabine (Romanized as Quinctilius), and he maximum probable symbolizes the people who buried their vain on Rome's outside hills. After transferring to a today's home close to the Forum, he built the Regia Palace and reigned thankfully for 40 3 years. According to Roman mythology, the priest-king ordered the community's spiritual life by way of manner of creating everyday cults and clergymen (flamines, pontifices, Salii, and the Vestal Virgins) and changing the calendar with the aid of the use of the usage of changing the 10-month 'Romulean' yr with a twelve-month three hundred and sixty five days. Some of the modifications may have befell in the end, making it no longer viable to take something at face rate. The Salian priests wore Bronze Age armor, suggesting an in advance enterprise agency, while the calendar alteration was maximum possibly made thru later Etruscan rulers. Some spiritual groups in Rome all through the regal age also can have been the cease end result of a robust man imposing modifications at the population, a exquisite deal as few could question Moses' presence however no longer attributing all Mosaic suggestions to him. Numa Pompilius can also have lived a extra real existence than his mythological adviser, the nymph Egeria.

The non violent Numa succeeded the militaristic Tullus Hostilius, who ruled for 32 years (673-642), defeating an Alban assault, destroying Alba, and shifting its humans to Rome.

Although there can be no archaeological proof of a catastrophic sacking of Alba inside the mid-seventh century, the shortage of the Iron Age civilization spherical this time can also have contributed to the narrative of Hostilius' deeds. The call Alban Mettius Fufetius, who succeeded the demise monarch as commander, can be traditionally massive. Mettius is the Latin equal of an Oscan magistrate referred to as meddix. Tullus Hostilius is venerated with the resource of a monument at the Curia Hostilia, the Senate's assembly area. The Hostilii did not benefit consulship or prominence until the second one century, lengthy after the Curia changed into installation and Tullus end up admitted to the royal canon, giving the king significant clout.

Ancus Marcius, like his predecessor Hostilius, sprung from plebeians and rose to the position of consul in 357 BC. There are functionality motives for Ancus' ancient accuracy. The monarch modified into each clever in peace and ambitious in combat. While a number of his exploits have been overstated to benefit the Marcian own family, he is credited for stretching Roman rule to Ostia at the mouth of the Tiber. According to records, he did no longer assemble a colony there, however instead took manipulate of the salt pans south of the river, vying with the Etruscans who controlled the north monetary institution and the Tiber bridge at Fidenae above Rome. The salt may be exchanged with the eastern tribes, however it had to pass the Tiber. Ancus is meant to have constructed Rome's first bridge certainly out of timber (sublica that means 'pile'). Its manufacturing can also had been related to the pontifices, frequently referred to as 'bridge-developers'. According to mythology, Ancus might also additionally have set up a bridgehead at the Janiculum hill to guard the salt route and his new bridge, however did now not consist of it into Rome. Tarquinius visited Rome at some point of his rule.

Chapter 3: The Roman Republic Government

During the 5th century, Rome confronted monetary hassle further to social and political upheaval, with the repercussions of the Tarquins' exile dominating the number one half of of the century. The Struggle of the Orders, a social, political, and monetary warfare a number of the patrician elite and the rest of Roman society, spanned hundreds of the fifth and fourth centuries.

Ancient assets for this time are although difficult, along side money owed through Livy and Dionysios of Halicarnassus and comments through unique historians of the past due Republic and empire. Many parts in their memories are suspicious and cannot be relied upon. Although Roman traditions approximately the fifth century may moreover encompass some historic facts, most of the cloth has a amazing deal of anachronism, subsequent explanation, and mythologizing. One most important problem is the dependability and validity of the fasti, magistrate lists, and military achievements granted. These are preserved in a whole lot of assets, which embody inscribed lists commissioned via Emperor Augustus.

In Roman way of lifestyles, the transition from monarchy to republic grow to be seen as a super transformation, regular with historic political idea. Despite the rhetoric and portrayal of Brutus as a liberator, there remained plenty continuity a number of the monarchy and the early republic. The king's authority (imperium) survived, but in location of being managed via a unmarried guy for lifestyles, it turn out to be held through the use of elected magistrates who served for a one-365 days term.

It seems that one or greater chosen yearly magistrates succeeded the monarch because the Roman kingdom's important leaders, protecting imperium (electricity of command), important armies, presided over senate and assembly gatherings, and exercising civil and criminal authority. Imperium changed into important to the top magistracies because it served as the foundation for civil and army authority, similarly to the right to command. Magistrates additionally had non secular responsibilities, and a citizen can also furthermore have had the proper to appeal inside the route of arbitrary motion taken via a magistrate in competition to them.

The amount of each year magistrates, their titles, and their interactions with each other are all complicated issues. The person of the leader Justice of the Peace can also have changed within the 5th century. Rome end up previously managed by means of manner of a unmarried preeminent Justice of the Peace, who changed into assisted thru the usage of one or greater lesser ones. The most senior magistrates in the early Republic had been known as praetors, no longer consuls. An historical each 12 months rite in which a magistrate known as the praetor maximus located a nail into the wall of the Capitolian temple to mark the 12 months shows that the praetor maximus have become Rome's maximum senior Justice of the Peace in the early Republic.

The dictator turn out to be each different Justice of the Peace who momentarily wielded final authority. The dictatorship modified into an historic post in Latinium, further to the normal top magistracy in Lanuvium and Aricia, in the end it is probably that Rome have become previously ruled by means of an each yr elected dictator. However, matters all of sudden changed. For the majority of the Republic, the dictator modified into an top notch Justice of the Peace decided on to rule Rome in times of country wide emergency and serving for simply six months, albeit having exquisite powers.

The difficult combination of consuls, praetors, dictators, and consular tribunes indicates that systems of authority in Rome in the fifth century remained changeable. Except in years at the same time as there have been faculties of consular tribunes, the fasti indexed magistrates each yr; even though, historians and antiquarians can also have compelled this shape at the document to convey early statistics steady with later exercise. The nice we will tell is that Rome modified into administered by elected every year magistrates in the 5th century, most in all likelihood in particular numbers and with numerous titles.

Significant dispositions came about within the course of Rome's early Republic, which includes the formation of a university element and the imposition of a set term limit. These thoughts, which constrained private authority, were achieved to the majority of anciliary magistracies hooked up later to guide the consuls. In the early 5th century, those helpers have been quaestors, which improved to four in 421.

During the fifth and fourth centuries, extra magistracies have been installation, collectively with the aedile and a modern day form of praetor.

These tendencies ended in authority being allocated greater frivolously some of the elite, in vicinity of being centered within the palms of a unmarried man for life. Access to energy grow to be a contentious hassle at some degree in the 5th and fourth centuries, with many jail, social, and political rights being restricted to a tiny elite. One of the distinguished storylines of the late fifth and early fourth centuries changed into the fight of numerous companies internal Rome for get entry to to strength and privilege.

The senate, which had large effect sooner or later of the center and later Republic, is further unknown. The formal collective manner of deal with used by senators way that it became an advisory body fabricated from the heads of top notch families, even though club also can have been more restricted. The later senate modified into greater professionally organized and covered people who matched without a doubt considered one of a kind qualifications for starting and money and have been effectively elected to magistracies. However, political institutions have been more bendy inside the 5th century, making rigid formal requirements brilliant.

The feature of the fifth-century senate is in addition unknown. It most possibly started out out due to the truth the king's advisory council and continued to serve in a consultative and non-government ability while the monarchy fell. Despite its crucial position within the Republic and feature an impact on over all additives of presidency, it in no manner had big authentic authority. Its choices had been handiest statements of opinion or propose, and it lacked direct governmental authority or the functionality to collect until summoned by way of manner of manner of a determine. At its top, the Senate modified into a smaller body with fewer senators and masses much less ethical energy.

How The Republic Expansion Started

The Plebeians, who have been gaining strength, suffered economic difficulties and were indebted to the Patricians, who sponsored the bulk of the loans in Rome. In 287 B.C., the Plebeians sought debt remedy from the Senate, but it modified into denied. As a final consequences, they seceded to Janiculum Hill and installation Quintus Hortensius as dictator. Hortensius enacted the Hortensian Law, which eliminated the Patricians' right to veto Plebeian law.

The Plebeians now held the de facto proper to end up Rome's censor or dictator. Within a few a long time, Rome had its first plebeian dictator and praetor, Q. Pubillius Philo. The Plebeian tribunes have been crucial pals to Patrician senators, making the Tribune an essential publish for formidable people searching for to beautify up the political ladder.

These political upheavals reshaped Roman society, making it more socially flexible. Men with sizable ambition and man or woman might probably sometimes collect high positions. The governing elegance advanced proper into a Patricio-Plebeian class, with a restrained variety of Plebeian households preserving the same social repute as previous Patrician families. With Plebeians having access to more of the spoils of struggle, those lower-caste people have been capable of finance steeply-priced elections and the social graces vital to climb in Rome.

Conflicts with neighboring tribes have fashioned Rome from its inception. During the Republic, those nearby fights helped to defend Rome and unfold its authority properly past the metropolis walls, ultimately spreading over the entire Italian peninsula. Rome commenced out its growth into Italy within the first century of the Republic, within the 5th century B.C., with one of the first vital engagements being the Battle of Lake Regillus in the direction of the Latin League.

Rome's authority over the Volsci and Aequi tribes became strengthened with the useful resource of the Battle of Corbione, which located Rome in the direction of the Aequi over again. Before the ultimate war amongst Rome and the Aequi, Rome fought the ambitious Etruscan town of Veii in the war of the Cremera. Despite loss, Rome in the end subdued all nearby tribes, setting it in a more potent function to confront distinct neighborhood risks, which include the Apennine hill tribes.

In the fourth century B.C., Rome faced a powerful foe within the Gallic tribes who've been invading Italy from the north. The Gallic troops had advanced similarly into the

North, invading important Etruscan towns. To guard those Etruscan friends, Rome modified into compelled to build up and engage in fight with the Gauls. The Battle of the Allia River came about between 390 and 387 B.C., and the day changed into seen as a bad portent for Rome.

Despite Rome's 15,000 warriors, the Gauls beat them and chased them decrease again to the metropolis gates. The Gauls and their chief, Brennus, efficiently sacked Rome. Anecdotes from the siege encompass the account of M. Manilus, a soldier and former Consul who valiantly battled the Gauls and vanquished them with the assist of later reinforcements.

The sacking of Rome is arguable, with some claiming the Romans drove the Gauls out with a military offensive, at the same time as others say they triumphed best after imparting the Gauls a sizable fee to leave the town. Regardless, the Gauls is probably a first-rate obstacle to Rome's attempts to extend its have an impact on over Italy.

Rome then clashed with the Samnites, fighting them for four a long time at the middle of the fourth century. During the First Samnite War, Rome decisively defeated the Samnites however turned into no longer succesful to complete the conquest due to an additional warfare with the Latins, whom Rome defeated at each the Battle of Vesuvius and the Battle of Trifanum. This diversion labored in Rome's choose, driving the Latins to subsequently surrender to its dominion.

Rome had a second possibility to triumph over the Samnites at a few degree inside the Second Samnite War, which lasted a long time from 327 to 304 B.C., with the benefit moving swiftly from the Romans to the Samnites after which lower back yet again. By 304 B.C., Rome had received and concluded its conquest of the Etruscans of Italy.

With the majority of the Italian peninsula below its fingers, Rome became its bold gaze to the bigger Mediterranean region. Its first sizeable opponent in the Mediterranean might be Pyrrhus, a effective Greek commander. Although Pyrrhus had severa large wins in his operations closer to Rome, the bulk of them brought about such large losses for his side that they could not legitimately rely victors.

The forces may want to warfare for decades until the Battle of Beneventum in 275 B.C. Historians name this fight a draw, however Pyrrhus and his forces have been tired, so he made the closing desire to go away Italy for Greece. Rome's victory closer to Pyrrhus installed the Republic as a dominant stress inside the Mediterranean and displayed its functionality to behavior battle on a international scale. With all of Italy now underneath its manage and a robust army recognition, Rome may confront one in each of its maximum ambitious opponents so far—Carthage.

Expansion Through The First, Second and Third Punic Wars

The Punic Wars were a watershed second for Rome and the Mediterranean vicinity, with hundreds of hundreds of soldiers slaughtered on each factors. Queen Elissar, a Tyre princess, based Carthage, a prominent Mediterranean town. When her brother tried to consolidate power in the kingdom, Elissar fled to the North African seaside.

Carthage's origins were focused on a Queen, no longer Romulus. Queen Elissar, frequently known as Queen Dido inside the West, have become once a Tyrean princess. When her brother sought to solidify dominance through manner of killing her husband, she fled to the North African beach. She married her uncle, Acherbas, who had hundreds extra strength and wealth than either of the present day co-monarchs.

Elissar achieved an splendid undertaking defying the Tyrian fleet, threatening to sell off all of her coins into the ocean if her supply changed into seized. When the fleet determined to art work with Elissar, she sailed west along side her amazing fleet. Following a quick forestall in Cyprus, Elissar and her military reached North Africa, wherein she successfully created Carthage.

Queen Elissar begged a neighboring Libyan monarch for sufficient land to create a small city, and he granted her request. She reduce an ox's conceal into small strips and have become capable of encircle the complete hill of Byrsa, providing Carthage with enough land.

Carthage's resourcefulness, war, and passion have become logos of the metropolis, which ultimately dominated and thrived in the location. By the time of the

Roman Republic, Carthage become a thriving commercial enterprise port that played an essential function in Phoenician exchange throughout the Mediterranean. It changed into in particular essential to the Phoenician trade community because it served as a rest prevent and secure harbor among Phoenician settlements within the east and the Phoenicians' mineral wealth in Iberia.

Carthage's wealth came from grain, textiles, slaves, tin, silver, gold, and dyes. However, there may be little archeological proof for the Carthaginians and their Phoenician country these days, and the empire's very last annihilation through the Romans left minimum archaeological record.

The First Punic War, which began out in 264 B.C., pitted Rome towards Carthage for naval dominance within the Mediterranean. Carthage's army turned into expert and dominated the Mediterranean, at the identical time as Rome lacked similar skills on the open sea. The first maximum essential battle come to be the Battle of Agrigentum, wherein Rome received and took possession of the city. However, Carthage changed into able to flee due to a scarcity of belongings and illness on each factors.

Rome's most essential invention have become the corvus, a deliver-mounted assault bridge that allowed the Romans to leverage their squaddies sooner or later of sea battles. During the Battle of Mylae, corvi attached to Roman ships were powerful, assisting Rome in capturing the first 30 enemy ships they confronted. Carthage's most effective protection in opposition to the corvi-reinforced ships end up to interact in lengthy maneuvers, but they misplaced 20 extra ships before losing the conflict and retiring.

The next battlefield changed into Sicily, wherein Rome and Carthage struggled for control of key assets from the possibility element. Rome in the end acquired this land struggle, imparting it the pressure and incentive to invade North Africa. By attacking Carthage, Rome would possibly in all likelihood undermine Carthage's grip and strength in the Mediterranean. Rome collected a superb army to sail to North Africa, destroying 350 Carthaginian ships inside the Battle of Cape Economus.

Carthage recovered momentum thru hiring a mercenary named Xanthippus, who led a reconstituted Carthaginian army in competition to Rome in the Battle of Tunis, capturing Roman leader Regulus and slicing off Rome's number one supply direction.

The Second Punic War is arguably the most famous due to the involvement of a Carthaginian commander, Hannibal Barca, and his legendary day journey over the Alps. Hannibal have end up regarded as a powerful opponent of Rome, but his siege engines, designed to break and overcome

Rome's fortified walls, stopped him from seizing the city itself.

To recapitulate, the First and Second Punic Wars were massive clashes between Rome and Carthage, with Rome's naval dominance and Hannibal's strategic techniques gambling essential roles in the battle.

Chapter 4: The Rise of Augustus and Rome Transition to Power

His Early Life

Octavian changed into born Gaius Octavius on September 23, 63 BC, in Rome. His terrific-grandfather, Gaius Octavius, grow to be a military tribune at a few stage inside the Second Punic War.

His father, Gaius Octavius, had previously been Macedonia's governor. His mom, Atia, emerge as Julius Caesar's niece, therefore the little one Octavian is his superb-nephew.

Octavian came to Spain in forty six BC to assist Julius Caesar in his navy advertising campaign in the direction of Pompey the Great's last supporters for the duration of the Civil War.

Caesar seemed extremely joyful with Octavian, and on the identical time as he decrease again to Rome, he modified his will to make him the inheritor to his riches and estates.

On March 15, forty four BC, Julius Caesar grow to be assassinated, igniting a few other civil warfare.

At the age of 18, Octavian again to Rome to clearly be given his position as Caesar's inheritor, as stipulated in his will.The Senate acquainted the selection, and in honor of his overdue uncle, Octavian took the decision Gaius Julius Caesar.

So, no matter the reality that we name him Octavian, he was referred to as 'Gaius Julius Caesar' throughout his life.In order to discover and punish his first rate-uncle's murders, Octavian original a political and navy alliance with specific effective Roman human beings.Octavian, Antony, and Lepidus founded the Second Triumvirate in 40 three BC.

Following Julius Caesar's dying in January 40 BC, the Senate topped him god.This no longer best served as a public monument to the dictator's reminiscence, but it additionally gave Octavian a modern-day claim to strength and grandeur.

He modified into now not most effective Caesar's son, but additionally the "son of a god".

The 3 guys then went out to arrest Caesar's assassins and punish them accountable. After a sequence of skirmishes, the hunt got here to a end at the Battle of Phillipi in October forty two BC.

During this warfare, the Second Triumvirate defeated the assassination's famed leaders, Brutus and Cassius. Octavian, Antony, and Lepidus now had usual control in Rome.

To display the strength in their bond, Octavian married his sister, Octavia, to Mark Antony in October 40 BC.

The First and Second Settlement

The partnership of Octavian, Antony, and Lepidus turned into brief-lived, as each attempted to rule the Roman republic and build their personal energy bases. Lepidus battled closer to Pompeiian rebels within the western Mediterranean, while Mark Antony moved to the japanese Mediterranean. Octavian focused on Italy and Rome, leaving Lepidus with little political or navy have an impact on. This left Octavian and Antony as Rome's pinnacle leaders, raising the possibility of each other civil war.

Mark Antony, who had a public infatuation with Cleopatra, became accused of neglecting his duties in Rome and dishonoring his sister. Octavian replied with the aid of manner of manner of divorcing Mark Antony in 32 BC. Octavian accused Antony of wishing to be a king, noting his moves in Egypt and desire to be buried there.

In 32 BC, the Senate disadvantaged Antony of his titles and released warfare on Cleopatra. The Senate desired Octavian, sparking civil struggle. The guys's armies and ships clashed in the Battle of Actium in 31 BC, with Octavian's troops victorious. Antony and Cleopatra escaped to Egypt and committed suicide in 30 BC, setting up Octavian as Rome's unchallenged ruler.

The First Settlement of 27 BC modified into a watershed 2nd in Roman facts, signaling the prevent of the dictatorship and the start of the Roman Empire. Following Mark Antony's defeat and demise, Octavian grow to be left with main a state that have been wrecked with the useful resource of a few years of civil war. Octavian had formerly managed his provinces with direct dictatorial powers, but after the priority of war passed, many Romans decided he not desired such absolute powers. On January 27, BC, Octavian selected to relinquish his absolute powers and hand them as much as the Senate. However, the Senate decided that it grow to be in Rome's splendid interests to permit Octavian to hold a number of his powers as a way to keep away from destiny civil struggle.

The First Settlement gave Octavian personal electricity over the provinces of Spain, Gaul, and Syria for 10 years, in addition to his land in Egypt, which he had received in 30 BC. This gave him the bulk of military authority, and he have emerge as granted the name of 'Augustus', thereby setting up him because of the reality the primary Roman emperor. In alternate, he promised numerous phrases, which includes sharing power with the Senate, not becoming king, and restoring the Republic after his lack of life.

From 31 until 23 BC, Augustus held one of the consulships on an annual basis, giving him more power to manipulate Rome. However, in 23 BC, Augustus have end up sick, and plenty of senators have been involved that he may want to die.

Fortunately, Augustus recovered, but the Senate required a 2d spherical of "settlements" to put together for the imperial succession.

The Second Settlement emerge as reached in 23 BC, on the same time as it become resolved that Augustus might in all likelihood stand apart as one of the consuls as quickly as a 12 months. However, he must maintain all the consul's (imperium) rights even as now not having to occupy the interest. He would possibly use this energy and the army authority that came with it for the rest of his life. To show that Augustus' imperium trumped all others, the Senate gave him the find out of imperium maius procunsulare, which translates to "perfect army commander."

As part of this accord, he changed into additionally granted the 'strength of a tribune' (tribunicia potestas), which enabled him to summon the Senate at any time, advise new criminal recommendations, and overturn any choice made by using the usage of manner of the Senate that he disagreed with (referred to as veto). This functionality to wield the powers of the tribuneship and consulship with out preserving the positions have become a cunning approach of exploiting traditional republican political structures.

His Achievements with Rome

Augustus' reign is referred to as the 'golden generation'. This emerge as because of the truth Augustus finished so much at some point of his reign.

During Augustus' reign, Rome have come to be a non violent and wealthy empire. Augustus resolved most of the problems that arose all through the Civil War technology.

He stepped forward the economic gadget and dealt with piracy and crime. Augustus furthermore enlarged his empire. He completed this with the useful resource of way of conquering new areas and forging agreements with specific nations.

Additionally, Augustus greater appropriate infrastructure. He built roads and canals to facilitate trade within the empire. He moreover constructed numerous public structures, including temples and theaters. Augustus also restructured the navy. He separated it into two components: legions stationed inside the provinces and the Praetorian Guard, which become primarily based absolutely in Rome.

Augustus' reign modified into so a fulfillment that it installed the sample for destiny Roman emperors. Augustus aimed to interchange authority to his son with a view to ensure succession. However, Augustus had no son of his very very own, so he needed to hunt for some different successor.

Augustus married his daughter, Julia, to his close to pal Marcus Agrippa, who end up a long time her senior.

Agrippa's sons have been consequently appointed Augustus' heirs. However, both sons died earlier than assuming electricity, leaving Augustus inside the equal state of affairs as previously.

Augustus then determined Tiberius, the son of his spouse Livia Drusilla from a previous marriage, as his successor. Tiberius modified into compelled to divorce his present partner, Vipsania Agrippina, so as for the present day marriage to take vicinity.

Augustus died on August 19, AD 14, quickly earlier than the age of seventy six. While there had been rumors of poisoning, it seems that naturally he died from natural causes. Tiberius succeeded him as Emperor.Augustus proved to be a remarkably capable leader. Despite the violence and conflict that defined his ascent to electricity, his almost forty-three hundred and sixty 5 days reign as Rome's ideal chief turn out to be significantly non violent in assessment to the century of civil conflict that preceded him. It remains uncertain how he finished this accomplishment.

As an instantaneous final effects of his achievement, Roman rulers for the following hundred years were frequently in evaluation to Augustus. Each of them could be expected to act in addition and reap similar ranges of navy, cultural, and monetary fulfillment.

However, it modified into an now not possible criterion to satisfy. Everyone in all his successors will in no way in shape his first rate duration in energy. Regardless of the restrictions that Rome confronted following his dying, Augustus' rule modified into so inexperienced that the Roman Empire remained in massive component unchanged.

Chapter 5: The Five Good Emperors

The name "Five Good Emperors" refers to Roman emperors seemed for their highly solid and wealthy reign, in addition to their attempts to reform authorities and control. They were portrayed as perfect rulers in the course of data, thru manner of authors of the time (consisting of Cassius Dio) and great characters of the Renaissance and Early Modern eras (at the side of Machiavelli and Edward Gibbon).

Collectively they are considered to have supervised the amazing technology of peace and prosperity that the Roman Empire expert - what Cassius Dio called as a "Kingdom of Gold" underpinned via amazing administration and smart insurance.

The Nerva-Antonine Dynasty (96 AD - 192 AD), the Roman Empire's 1/three dynasty, have become certainly liable for the Five Good Emperors. They protected the dynasty's founder, Nerva, further to his successors Trajan, Hadrian, Antoninus Pius, and Marcus Aurelius.

These made up all but of the Nerva-Antonine Dynasty, with Lucius Verus and Commodus excluded from the renowned five. This is because of the fact Lucius Verus ruled alongside Marcus Aurelius but did now not stay prolonged, at the same time as Commodus added the dynasty and the "kingdom of gold" to an untimely stop.

Indeed, after Commodus' disastrous administration, the empire modified into regarded to have slid into a normal but irreversible crumble, with occasional glimmers of preference, however in no way to rise to the heights of the Nerva-Antonines. While emperors had been removed at the time, a records of the Five Good Emperors includes facts on the Nerva-Antonine Dynasty.

Nerva (30 - ninety eight AD)

Nerva, born in AD 30, changed right into a key player in past due Republican and early Imperial politics. His faraway own family ties to the Julio-Claudians and shortage of navy enjoy earned him a valued function as a counselor to diverse imperial courts. Under Nero's reign, Nerva executed an vital issue in foiling Piso's plot and become rewarded for his offerings. He maintained a sturdy connection with destiny emperor Vespasian and turn out to be selected as his junior consul in AD seventy one.

Nerva served as an adviser at some point of the Flavian eras of Vespasian, Titus, and Domitian. Following Saturninus' legionary riot in opposition to Domitian, Nerva turn out to be promoted to normal consul and given precise gratitude for coming across the conspiracy. However, goodwill did now not persist during Domitian's reign, and Nerva seemed to be prone to being singled out with the resource of the emperor's conspiracy theories.

By the mid-90s AD, there was sufficient proof to reveal that Domitian had distanced himself from Nerva, and only horoscopes forecasting Nerva's imminent dying saved Domitian from attacking his adviser. The killings of other senators and intimate court docket docket advisers at some point of Domitian's "reign of terror" forced the final individuals of his court docket to behave.

Domitian have turn out to be assassinated thru members of his personal home staff on September 18, AD 96, and Nerva have become Emperor. Nerva's characteristic and fast nomination to gain fulfillment Domitian can also had been brought on by means of using manner of personal ambition, however as a renowned senior statesman of the Senate and a member of the Flavian allies, his selection supplied a brief and easy hazard.

Nerva's preference grow to be typically inspired through the present day emperor's age, because of the reality he turned into supposedly in unwell fitness and without direct male successors. Military aspirants for the imperial throne identified that Nerva's appointment come to be a temporary diploma, and that the actual sport is probably gained with the aid of Nerva's successor.

The loss of existence of Domitian in Ancient Rome brought about complications for Nerva's authorities, because of the fact the Praetorians had been outraged and desired revenge. Nerva became forced to give up the Praetorian prefects inner a yr of his arrival, however the Senate welcomed their go once more to political prominence. Nerva's first response to their needs included refraining from murdering Senate people, releasing political prisoners, returning exiles, and reimbursing a few assets. He additionally repealed the 'Jewish tax' and approved the prosecution of political spies, which regarded to bridge the divide amongst opposing agencies however ultimately necessitated his involvement.

Nerva sought to emulate Augustus' governing style, but relied on his personal body of workers for the majority of imperial administrative obligations. He maintained the treasury with the resource of the use of elevating taxes to stability his prices, limiting immoderate actual religious events, sports activities activities sports activities, and gala's, and putting in location 'alimentary establishments'. With the exception of Hadrian's reign, those popular duties persisted till Marcus Aurelius' lack of existence.

Nerva's public works report suffered because of his quick reign, no matter the truth that he constructed the Nerva Forum, maintained street advent plans, and repaired flood harm to the Colosseum. He nominated Sextus Julius Frontinus as curator of the water supply, supplying records on the antique Roman water gadget.

The emperor's navy talents had been handicapped with the aid of a lack of formal education or enjoy, as seen with the resource of the Praetorian's early condemnation. Nerva's marvel succession plan ensured actual imperial safety. Trajan changed into officially identified as his adoptive successor in October AD ninety seven, and with one stroke of brilliance, volatile ranges of political dissension had been eliminated. Trajan's prolonged data of determination and employer to the empire made him arguably the handiest feasible candidate for the constant continuance of Imperial strength.

Despite his quick 16-month tenure, Nerva's legacy turn out to be the genius of his succession plan. Trajan got here to electricity with a army history that he could placed to suitable use over the subsequent severa a few years, and his familiar a achievement leadership is often seemed as 2d high-quality to Augustus due to the fact the wonderful of the Roman Emperors.

Trajan (fifty 3 - 117 AD)

Trajan, born Marcus Ulpius Trajanus in Italica, have become a a success Roman emperor and the number one "provincial" ruler from outside of Italy. During his reign, the Roman Empire grew, triumphed inside the Dacian Wars, and conquered the Kingdom of Armenia. Trajan is well-known for his public works, together with the constructing of Trajan's Column and the growth of the port of Ostia.

Trajan's father, Vespasian, grow to be the primary within the family line to benefit a Senate seat, and he rose to the consulship within the path of the chaotic length after Nero's death. He served below Vespasian in Judaea earlier than moving right now to turn out to be governor of Baetica, Syria, and Asia Minor. Trajan observed in his father's footsteps, acquiring positions via the same old 'cursus honorum' manner, with a large emphasis on the army.

Domitian appointed Trajan as Legate of Legio VII Gemina in Hispania Tarraconensis, and he rallied its guys to shield the besieged emperor closer to Saturninus' rebellion in 89 AD. Trajan's love for Domitian may also additionally were a small supply of embarrassment whilst the emperor turn out to be assassinated.

Trajan turn out to be the catalyst for Nerva's manipulate and the clean transfer of power between the Flavians and the so-referred to as 'Five Good Emperors' even as Domitian died in 96 AD. Trajan maintained a genial approach together together with his men, steadily winning them over.

Before returning to Rome in 99 AD, Trajan hung out surveying enemy positions and investigating Danube fortifications. Decebalus, the Dacian King, strengthened his country, supplying a excessive chance to Roman authority. Trajan had no choice but to layout a plan to eliminate the danger. He endorsed for a sincerely low-key approach to governing, letting provincial governors make their personal choices and wonderful deferring to the emperor in severe occasions.

Trajan pursued popular policies that punished delators, curtailed the authority of Praetorians, and changed the judicial gadget. The humans dubbed him Optimus, that means first-class, in reputation of his efforts to hold and decorate the alimenta social help tool. By the spring of 101 AD, plans were finished, and the emperor marched north with an military that might ultimately range as lots as 11 legions.

The Dacian War blanketed both grueling battles and technological wonders. Trajan triumphed due to the Roman navy's well-known hassle and fortitude. The Romans constructed massive roadways alongside the Danube with the help of engineer Apollodorus of Damascus, overcoming demanding situations and threatening terrain.

After a decisive victory at Tapae in a single 0 one AD, Trajan ordered the erection of an altar similarly to the observance of annual funeral customs. The Romans advanced on the Dacian capital, compelling Decebalus to submit. Trajan decrease once more to Rome to commemorate his short triumph, which acquired him the discover Dacicus.

Trajan, the Roman emperor, faced several annoying situations for the duration of his reign, consisting of losses by way of using way of Domitian and Decebalus. He come to be capable of rebuild his military and protection structures unopposed. Trajan's engineer, Apollodarus, built the arena's longest stone bridge to move the Danube. In one 0 5 AD, the Romans fought a new conflict, and Trajan led them to victory over Dacia. The combat ended at the same time as the Romans arrived on Sarmizegethusa, but Decebalus changed into compelled to go away and commit suicide. Dacia became diagnosed as an imperial province, and numerous new colonies had been normal, establishing the framework for Roman rule that maintains to at the prevailing time. Trajan left inside the lower lower back of monuments to have amusing his victory: the Tropaeum Traiani and Trajan's Column. Trajan arrived in Rome in 106 AD with a top notch quantity of 5 million gold and two times that a whole lot silver, permitting him to keep the imperial treasury and fund initiatives. Trajan's recognition a number of the people and elite encouraged Indian embassies to pay him homage.

Trajan's administrative control noticed a resurgence of exceptional individuals of the circle of relatives with the aristocracy, as he allocated governing power and centered on centralizing the Roman government in desire to tolerating corruption. He best held the consulship six times, however he did it honorably, with many friends and allies serving many phrases. Trajan predicted financial officers to perform similarly to military subordinates, the usage of their discretion for almost all of selections and filing to the emperor first-rate at the same time as truly required.

Trajan turned into no longer a reformer, however he observed out the importance of Latin and Italian history for the empire's regular fitness. The alimentary device, which furnished food and special requirements, multiplied delivery costs in Rome and Italy. Trajan moreover recounted the troops' inclination inside the path of savagery thru social endeavors.

Trajan funded imperial architectural obligations along with Trajan's Forum, Markets, and Imperial Baths. He fostered trade throughout the empire by way of the usage of extending ports and constructing highways, together with the Via Traiana.

Trajan's reign become amazing for the inclusion of women in imperial public life, collectively alongside with his partner and sister being taken into consideration favorably and identified for their offerings to the empire.

Emperor Trajan, irrespective of his home achievements, end up a military soldier at coronary heart. Rome's growth into the east, which encompassed Syria and Arabia Petraea, placed it in a position to govern key commercial business enterprise routes some of the east and west. Armenia's lengthy-popularity political war with Rome and the Parthian Empire culminated in 113 AD, whilst Parthia positioned a candidate on the throne without Roman authorization.

The Parthian War shattered the already shaky peace among Rome and Parthia, inflicting Trajan to withdraw east of Rome on the identical time as assembling an invasion pressure. In 114 AD, he marched into Armenia, conquering locations like

Babylon and Ctesiphon, annexed Mesopotamia and Assyria as Roman provinces, and acquired the pick out out Parthicus.

Trajan continued to march southeast, in the long run achieving the Persian Gulf in 116 AD. However, the prolonged-term possibilities for Roman rule were questionable. In 117 AD, the Romans suffered their first defeat of the battle, with Trajan barely fending off personal threat. The rise up unfold to Jewish settlements in Egypt, Cyrene, and Cyprus, culminating in giant slaughter of Roman humans and the destruction of pagan temples.

Trajan became sick in the path of the summer time of 117 AD and died at Selinus on August nine, 117 AD. Hadrian, Trajan's son, have turn out to be properly-favored by manner of the Empress Plotina, however his ascension went unchallenged whilst Trajan have come to be unwell. Trajan used power with a top notch deal plenty less strict authority, garnering the respect of each the humans and the nobles.

Chapter 6: Political Instability
Economy Decline

By Hadrian's reign, Rome had ceased growing. Hadrian did this as a precaution, believing that the Empire could not useful resource further increase. The slowdown in boom has substantial economic effects. Rome's reliance on conquered peoples and their related tithes and taxes introduced approximately a immoderate financial loss. As a final results, Rome had restrained assets to guide its huge navy. War changed into beneficial to the Roman Empire's monetary tool.

To address this trouble, Rome issued the Edict of Caracalla in 212, moreover referred to as the Constitutio Antoniniana. The edict granted complete Roman citizenship to all loose person guys inside the Empire, similarly to identical rights without spending a dime girls. While a few argue that this modified into a social rule geared toward balancing a numerous populace, historians recollect it become thru and big intended to elevate tax earnings for the usa, that can then be used to fund an increasing army. This decree had a long-term impact on the Empire, decreasing stigma and imparting authority to foreigners.

Despite incurring initial prices in troops and substances, key possessions like Dacia generated extensive returns in natural resources. The machine relied cautiously on slave hard work from the far off provinces to live to tell the tale. As the slave change dwindled, Rome wanted a modern financial model to maintain its massive frame of human beings.

The colonato served as an opportunity to slave hard paintings. This shape installation the feudal tool of vassals, which ruled Europe for some time. The difficult paintings model separated large estates into smaller portions for tenant farmers. Tenant farmers had vital factors and authority over their belongings, but had been required to pay excessive taxes to the estate proprietors. The property holders benefited from free hard paintings at the same time as furthermore receiving reimbursement. Thousands of metropolis terrible migrated to the rural monetary device as a ultimate inn.

The colonial machine expanded riches for landowners. The Roman tax collectors were unable to accumulate taxes from the rich elite, leading to a loss of profits for the Roman economic tool.

Corruption have come to be a high hassle in Rome's paperwork, particularly following the Diocletian reforms. The reforms aimed to interrupt up and conquer the Empire, making it greater controllable. They exacerbated the complexity and corruption of Rome's office work.

Diocletian set up a Tetrarchy, dividing the Empire into 4 quadrants as his first sizeable flow into. The concept proposes Augusti because the essential "emperors" within the East and West of the Empire. A Caesar should oversee each half of the Empire, reporting to the Augusti ruling beauty. Augusti positions have been held by the use of manner of Constantinus inside the east and Galerius inside the west.

To restrict nearby governors' have an effect on, provinces have been divided into smaller portions. Thirteen dioceses were mounted to supervise the provinces. Each diocese was led via the usage of the use of a vicarius, who stated to a Praetorian prefect below one of the Tetrarchs.

Diocletian additionally dealt with monetary changes. Prior to these changes, Rome's silver currency were severely depreciated, threatening the entire economic gadget. Diocletian issued the Edictum De Priviis Rerum Venalium to cope with monetary worries. The decree installed fee barriers to save you immoderate speculation within the Roman exchange network.

The Diocletian reforms stepped forward Roman paperwork, main to greater functionality for corruption. According to a few estimates, the reforms resulted in a doubling of the paperwork, with one bureaucrat every 5000 residents.

Diocletian reforms had a huge effect on provincial government, which introduced about extended corruption. The changes shifted electricity from provincial governors to army dukes, who supervised many provinces simultaneously. Although the intention become to reduce the political class's dominance, it as a substitute elevated the electricity of the landed gentry. Governors underneath the colonial, proto-feudal regime lacked have an impact on over the ruling elite and have been unable to successfully call for taxes. The estate proprietors sought political agendas primarily based mostly on their economic sources.

The Downfall of Trade and Poverty

Rome had monetary hardships, collectively with hyperinflation and foreign exchange devaluation. The navy's increase prompted a downward spiral. Emperors need to buoy the

To pay their military and protect their rule, the Romans devalued their coins with less expensive metals like copper and bronze, causing inflation.

Understandably, this resulted in a large increase in pricing. Diocletian's reforms came at a time at the identical time as the Roman financial gadget became near catastrophe. By the near of the 1/3 century AD, at some point of the Crisis that in the end introduced about Rome's downfall, the silver denari had little price. Trade became restrained to retail coinage, ensuing in an untraceable financial device.

The impact on the Roman Empire's business network have come to be extremely good. The Empire depended on trade amongst Mediterranean ports and routes connecting Rome's territory. For years, traders depended on those highways for green motion during the Empire. Rare Syrian commodities had been as handy as Spanish merchandise on the ones paths.

This numerous community have become one of the maximum flourishing and complicated economic structures within the global, and have become now not exceeded till the contemporary device emerged in contemporary a few years.

By the Third Century Crisis, the devalued overseas cash made pass-border alternate and change a nightmare. Civil upheaval along those roads made buying and selling hazardous and inconsistent. Large assets owners targeted on subsistence cultivation and nearby trade. Estates began generating their very personal items in location of relying on imports from big towns during the Empire.

The Roman economic device skilled every devaluation and decentralization. Large estates have become separate fiefdoms that did no longer benefit society. The new monetary model set up a precedent for Europe, main to centuries of dominance through the manorial monetary machine. As metropolis terrible and tradesmen faced fewer opportunities, they had been more and more reliant on the landed aristocracy, ensuing in increased strength and riches for oligarchs. As the operating horrible misplaced their independence and privileges as Roman citizens, the society have become increasingly more risky and class war increased.

The fragmented Roman financial system driven authority eastward to Asia Minor. Diocletian picked Nicomedia as his headquarters and sent his 2nd-in-command to the Italian Peninsula. This change foreshadowed the emergence of the East because of the truth the Western Roman Empire declined.

All of this placed immoderate strain on the Emperor's estates and troops. Furthermore, the Emperor now held the

The undertaking of walling in specific metropolis-fashion fiefdoms throughout the empire at excessive charge. The wealthy aristocracy and faraway provinces did now not fear Rome and often prevented paying taxes. The decentralized economic tool shifted Roman authority from Rome to rural estates. The Roman Empire suffered financially, however it furthermore launched Europe on a course of financial break that persevered till the middle Ages, enslaving the commonplace man to wealthy landowners.

Chapter 7: The External Invaders

Apparently if Rome had simplest been attacked from inside, it would had been able to withstand. The Empire faced every external and internal annoying condition, leading to its inevitable crumble. The Germanic tribes, collectively with unique tribes similar to the Huns, posed the best danger to the Empire's protection.

Since Hadrian's time, Rome has followed a protective stance. Rome prioritized retaining its borders and current domain names, in region of increasing into new territories. This caused the upward thrust of powerful warring parties out of doors Rome's limitations. In the zero.33 century AD, migrations and invasions from northern tribes completely altered the Roman Empire. These moves lasted over 4 centuries and stimulated Europe even after the Roman Empire fell. Tribes fought in the direction of every super and Rome, reshaping the continent's way of life and identification.

Barbarians Invaders

The "barbarians" have been now not a homogeneous organization, but as an opportunity a set of numerous tribes from Northern Europe and Scandinavia. Around one thousand BC, Germanic peoples moved from southern Scandinavia and Germany to the area some of the Elbe and Oder rivers. By two hundred BC, a wave of migrants had unfold to the west and south, causing struggle with the Celts and using them to the Rhine earlier than settling in southern Germany. By 100 BC, the tribes had migrated to Roman and Cisalpine Gaul, in which they clashed with Caesar at some stage in the pre-Empire length.

A second wave of migration added Germanic tribes from northern Europe to the east, across the Baltic Sea and the Carpathians. These tribes were referred to as the Franks and Saxons after becoming a member of via army alliances and marriages.

The current-day-day idea of Germanic tribes is that they had been a frenzied warrior civilization, regardless of the truth that they have been virtually as superior as any way of life on the time. Goth tribes specialised in rings, seafaring, and agriculture. The lack of sophistication form in assessment to Rome can also have contributed to their label as "barbarian". In a Goth society, the impoverished have been no longer often omitted. According to positive historians, Romans who lived in Goth territory fared higher than those beneath Roman rule.

The Germanic hordes were identified for carrying skins even after assembly with Romans, which can also have contributed to their recognition as "wild" people. They had been regularly pagan till accepting the Arian form of Christianity inside the zero.33 century AD, manner to a diligent Gothic bishop who translated present Christian writings into their language.

Germanic tribes first of all clashed with Rome inside the late second century B.C. During this era, Roman Consul Gaius Marius fought toward tribes in Hispania, Gaul, and Italy. Julius Caesar utilized the concern of those battles to justify his annexation of Gaul a few years later. Rome faced those tribes at some stage in their enlargement into the Rhine and Danube areas. The interplay amongst those entities grow to be greater complicated in effective locations. Although there were armed battles, the Germanic tribes in those territories installed exchange and alliances with Rome.

In a hundred and one B.C., the Teutoni and Cimbri tribes entered the Italian Peninsula from the north. Caesar and one-of-a-type Roman commanders noticed Germanic tribes as a persistent chance that needed to be controlled. During Caesar's reign, the tribal lands of the Rhine and Danube have been called "Germania". Rome now had a regarded opponent. Caesar utilized the enemy to gain manual for the protection of Transalpine Gaul. Despite his achievements over the Germanic tribes, they remained resilient and had prolonged-lasting consequences on Rome.

In the first decade after Christ, a revolution broke out in Germania led via Arminius, who had previously been an ally of Rome. During the Battle of the Teutoburg Forest, he defeated three Roman legions with Publius Quinctillius Varus. The earliest confrontations among Rome and the tribes had a protracted-lasting effect on their dating. Within some a long time, the Germanic tribes have end up the maximum big danger to the Roman Empire.

Barbarians and the Empire

The barbarian invasions, which had been large population migrations in Romance languages, established that the Roman

Empire modified into not in decline at some diploma inside the fourth century. Contact a number of the empire and the barbarians, especially thru immigration into Roman territory, were underway for a few years in advance than 378. The Romans were aware of numerous areas and peoples out of doors the empire's obstacles, in particular the robust, modern-day, and in component Hellenized Persian Empire inside the east. The Persians had little preference to enter Roman territory and reside there, who pick to seize the empire's wealthy eastern provinces.

The conflict among the two civilizations changed into not between civilizations and barbarians, however among civilizations that had been preventing for a long term. The Tigris and Euphrates rivers separated the Romans, and they now and again received bridgeheads on the Tigris' further element. Deserts to the south, alongside its Arabian and African borders, provided protection for the empire. The locals were nomads, and the Romans had been preoccupied with ensuring no man or woman entered. The nomads traveled to and fro at some point of the empire's limitations, and the Romans made agreements with tribal chieftains to protect the barren region routes. The empire had no hassle coexisting with Bedouin and Berber nomads, and tribe chiefs had been supplied Roman citizenship and erected villas which have been basically fortifications.

The Rhine and Danube rivers described Rome's northern frontiers, and it have become idea that those natural boundaries stored the barbarians away. The maximum deadly barbarians the empire encountered dwelt on the opportunity aspect of those rivers, in a slew of tribes that the Romans from time to time attempted to catalog, categorize, and constitute. However, they observed little charge in variety and understood now not some thing approximately foreigners.

The geographic range decided within the barbarian hinterlands piqued the hobby of Roman authors, when you consider that data of such places modified into required whether or not deciding on a political path or organizing a navy day experience. Germania, placed east of the Rhine and north of the Upper Danube, end up a rustic of woodlands and marshes in which the Romans had burnt their palms many times. The Germans were familiar and nearly domestic, and their martial capabilities is probably used to the empire's gain.

The Romans had little expertise of what have turn out to be beyond the Danube boundary, especially within the territories throughout the river's mouth, wherein it runs into the Black Sea. There had been incredible steppes that stretched over Ukraine and led instantly to the plains of applicable Asia, the house of nomadic tribes that had descended in waves onto the exceptional, set up civilizations of China, India, and the Roman Empire.

The Germans on the alternative problem of the Rhine created lots a good deal less fear when you consider that that they'd continuously been farmers and lived in robust territories, with every tribe having its non-public canton. Relations with the Germans can be managed, however the steppe dwellers on the alternative aspect of the Danube instilled an extended manner greater terror in Roman hearts.

Fear completed a key role inside the Romans' mind-set in the direction of barbarians, as proven with the aid of ancient events at the aspect of Brennus and his Gauls occupying Rome in 387 BC and the hazard posed thru the Cimbri and Teutoni, whom Marius crushed in 102 BC. This trouble modified into bolstered by way of the usage of opinions from the Danubian plains, wherein the government have become compelled to evacuate citizens and skip refugees to keep away from nomad attacks. The African border also prompted lamentations from property proprietors who grumbled approximately the navy's ineffectiveness and threatened to arm their region employee's.

In the imperial palace, the ministers felt that the empire might also want to punish the barbarians for raising their heads too immoderate. They argued that if Rome needed to motel to interim solutions, it changed into due to limited sources, budgeting, and a lack of coins and troops. However, the barbarians remained warlike and needed regular punishment considering they in no manner learnt their lesson. After some years after their preceding loss, their bravery might possibly cross returned, and they'd penetrate imperial territory, raid farms, kidnap slaves, and seize the emperors. The emperors might be pressured to intrude and set up punitive expeditions, which intended that the Romans must invade enemy territory, burn towns, slaughter women and youngsters, steal cattle, and harm flora till tribe chieftains arrived and pleaded for forgiveness.

The massive assets owners and merchants who had complained approximately the lack of safety profited handsomely from the seized slaves, the required tributes imposed on the barbarian tribes, and the animals that the army again to the motherland and gave to the people. The huge belongings owners, who have been required to offer the navy with recruits picked from amongst their farmers, were extra than willing to pay a tax rather, for the cause that the army emerge as recruiting on the opposite detail of the boundary.

The fourth-century Romans recognized that the barbarians had been a valuable useful resource that needs to not be squandered. They got here to count on that the wretched wretches who entered the empire illegally and lived illegally were definitely fleeing hunger, suffering, and bloodshed from damaging tribes. As extended due to the fact the imperial authorities handled immigration without problems, with smooth felony recommendations and diligent tracking, the expanding range of immigrants did no longer produce problems or outcomes.

Chapter 8: The Fall of the Empire

Horrors of the Battle of Adrianople

The Huns had ousted the Goths, who sought protection within the Eastern Roman Empire, which emerge as ruled with the aid of way of Valens. They had been accepted to settle as foederati, which supposed they had to warfare for their position in the Empire. However, because of awful administration, many Goths were mistreated within the Empire, sparking a rise up. Valens asked help from the Western emperor, Gratian, who furnished the East with notable troops and a series of youngster conflicts most of the Goths and Rome.

Despite Rome's notable tries to quash the rebellion, the Goths have been not truly removed. Valens took over the Roman thing of the fight, summoning further forces from Syria and asking for Gratian's legions from Gaul. He accumulated a greater pressure in

Constantinople, whilst his 2nd, Sebastianus, collected in Adrianople.

Sebastianus had a few early fulfillment in opposition to the Goths, which fueled Valens' preference for combat. He marched his army toward Adrianople, at the same time as the Goths, led through Fritigern, marched 10,000 troops there. Valens resolved to enter combat with out searching beforehand to more troops from the West, oblivious to the huge military on the Roman side.

On August 9, Valens marched his soldiers to the Gothic stronghold on the metropolis's north side. The Roman navy came exhausted and dehydrated, and Fritigern diverted their hobby through the use of lighting fireside on the fields and negotiating the alternate of captives. The Romans have been perplexed via this, uninformed of the Gothic cavalry's approach and overconfident of their very own numbers.

The combat became a massacre, with Valens deserted via his deserting legions and cavalry. Some claim the emperor perished on the field or fled to a neighboring cottage. When the Goths came to raid the settlement, they set hearth to the home, ignorant that it contained a treasured potential captive. Valens' small domestic became destroyed thru fireside.

The Roman loss at Adrianople had a protracted way-accomplishing implications, due to the fact the barbarians have turn out to be formidable foes and the Roman army's mind-set to combat became reshaped. This brief-time period final results did not deliver the Empire down, however it changed proper into a key flaw in its armor and a foreshadowing of what have grow to be to return decrease back. Rome sought to divide administrative functions amongst severa regions of the Empire, which includes the Tetrarchy, but the imperator changed into never divided in the course of those durations.

Theodosius I may be taken into consideration the final emperor of the Roman Empire for the reason that he modified into the last to preside over a unified empire. From his reign in advance, the Roman Empire turned into irrevocably divided into components: Western and Eastern. Theodosius made severa good sized reforms, which includes putting in Nicene Christianity because of the truth the Empire's respectable faith and prohibiting pagan customs which include the Vestal Virgins and the Olympic Games. This growing position for Christianity assisted the separation of the location in , thinking about there has been loads debate over what was without a doubt orthodox in terms of religion.

The East and West had awesome financial and barbarian histories, making it suitable to installation Romes in area of honestly sharing administrative competencies. After Theodosius died in 395, the Empire changed into irretrievably divided amongst his sons, ensuing in horrible authorities and big anarchy. Stilicho, a very specific individual in Roman data, got here to prominence within the direction of this period, marrying Theodosius' niece and appearing as regent for Honorius after the empire's extermination. Stilicho modified right into a soldier who captivated Theodosius' hobby, turning into his right hand man and entrusted with the governance of the Western Empire after Honorius rose to the throne.

Goth and Rome

The Visigoths, or "Goths of the West," had lengthy brought on problems for the Western Empire. With Alaric's ascent, Stilicho and Western Rome found out they needed to respond fast, specially whilst Alaric violated the 2 countries' peace accord with the aid of manner of major an assault within the direction of Roman possessions in Thrace. Rufinus changed into out inside the Eastern Empire, directing the Huns' regular attacks on Roman territories inside the area. As a impact, he tried to barter with Alaric in man or woman, making the government within the Eastern court docket docket cautious of Rufinus and his picks. Stilicho became allowed to march eastward in competition to the Visigoths on my own. However, on the verge of triumph, Arcadius ordered Stilicho to retire, possibly driven by way of manner of the intrigue swirling at courtroom docket. Rufinus became assassinated thru his private men quickly after this departure, leaving the younger Arcadius to govern on my own.

Stilicho pressed on in his campaign in opposition to the Visigoths, undaunted. He marched against them all another time in Macedonia, reaching a decisive victory however failing to recognize the cunning Alaric. There are numerous reasons why

Alaric may moreover have slipped through Rome's draw close, alongside facet debauchery and partying on Stilicho's side, as well as the truth that Arcadius always despised Western soldiers in his domains and might have asked Stilicho to retire once more, fearing Stilicho had a watch at the location. One likely clarification end up an revolt in North Africa headed via Gildo, a Roman commander. Gildo wanted to capture Roman territory in Africa and circulate them to the Eastern a part of the Empire, depriving the West of a vital grain supply. Stilicho have emerge as in brief distracted and switched his cognizance to Africa, sending Gildo's brother to confront him in combat. Rome acquired, and Stilicho's have an impact on have emerge as even more potent after being chosen consul.

Stilicho requested in 406 that the rulers in Constantinople repair authority of East Illyricum to the Western Empire, which

Theodosius had administratively assigned to the East. He presupposed to take benefit of those areas as a strategic vantage component from which to release expeditions toward the Germanic tribes in cooperation with Alaric. The East refused, and in the end of 406, a coalition of Germanic tribes crossed the frozen Rhine to attack the territory of Roman Gaul. In reaction, a sequence of army revolts erupted sooner or later of the vicinity and in Britannia, severely negative Stilicho's photo as a commander. Constantine III of Britain taken into consideration this as an opportunity and launched his own upward push up. Stilichus' second, Sarcus, achieved a few success in opposition to Constantine III however changed into pressured to escape, leaving Stilichus to lessen off the Alps in a determined bid to save you an invasion of the Italian Peninsula.

Chapter 9: Roman Life and Culture

Agriculture and Warfare

Agriculture has grown to be the Roman humans' essential business agency, with peasant farmers serving as the spine of the kingdom. The sword earned Rome's conquest of Italy, and the plow cemented it. The excellent citizen of the early days has become characterized as a Cincinnatus or Manius Curius, who prepared their very personal herb-primarily based truely eating regimen. The early gala's of Rome, the supremacy of later rustic tribes over town tribes, and personal names like Fabius (Beanman) and Lentulus (Lentilman) all factor to the importance of agriculture.

Initially, agriculture have become now not taken into consideration as a manner for the kingdom to make use of Italy's natural riches. It changed into a circle of relatives problem overseen with the useful resource of paterfamilias, who were in charge of offering for his or her circle of relatives. The primary weight-reduction plan consisted of porridge made from floor meal, water, and salt, further to garden greens. Wheat and bread changed porridge within the 5th century, and that they had been delivered.

With the improvement of Roman peasant cultivation, older situations vanished in Italy as soon as Rome conquered it. The Greek towns of southern Italy have been part of the Hellenistic global's capitalist device, sending big grain to Greece, on the identical time as Etruria, Carthaginian Sicily, and Sardinia furnished Punic towns in Africa. Most Greek towns inside the south fell to Samnite tribes and Roman colonization, turning into peasant communities, resulting in Italy being generally a rustic of small farmers.

Rome's conquest of the Mediterranean had a primary monetary have an effect on on Italy, specially within the south. The nation had hundreds of property for customers, and the Hannibalic War induced a spike in land profits. Land have become a supply of hypothesis, and owners grew to end up it over to stewards. As conflicts added about a loss of free exertions, slave tough paintings supplanted it on huge estates. This precipitated a capitalist device of massive estates focused on pasturage, livestock elevating, or wine and olive agriculture. The absentee owners extended the ranks of the the Aristocracy and center splendor in Rome and exceptional Italian cities.

Cato's work on agriculture paints a vibrant picture of existence in Italy at this period. He promoted grazing because the most financial use of land, bringing up growing name for for horses, wool, and meat. He moreover campaigned for viticulture, vegetable gardens, olive plantations, fodder meadows, and grain manufacturing. The advent of slave exertions driven many free laborers off the land, resulting in a huge variety of jobless citizens. Tiberius Gracchus favored to provide them a sparkling start through encouraging them to go back to the land.

The early Roman navy become constructed on a citizen militia, which proved vain for navy goals. The Servian reform resulted within the formation of an army, with the 'country in arms' being the number one political assembly. The navy became cut up into devices, or legions, and pay became instituted during the siege of Veii. As Rome's territory and populace grew, two consular armies with legions each have been usual. Experience, competence, and age changed coins and the census because the foundations of military employer. The heavy infantry have come to be separated into three strains: hastati, , and triarii, however slight-armed guys have been despite the fact that recruited thru a inflexible census tool. The legion grow to be split into 30 maniples, each with one hundred twenty infantrymen, to offer more flexibility than the phalanx's mass-strategies. The pilum, a 6 1/2-foot-extended javelin made from half wood and half of of iron, supplanted the spear in the the front traces. The set up infantry of Rome changed into advanced into right cavalry, regardless of the fact that the Romans depended increasingly on their allies.

The Roman navy, which conquered Italy, have emerge as restructured in advance than conquering the Mediterranean. The rigid phalanx and battle-line had been insufficiently flexible, resulting in legions collapsing and Roman cavalry failing to perform. Scipio Africanus, the first Roman commander, set up his new edition navy in Spain, forming lines that labored autonomously and adopting the Spanish sword and pilum. This resulted internal the arrival of Roman strategies which consist of cohorts, which in the end advanced into devices.

The Hannibalic battle professionalized the Roman military, however many soldiers again to civilian lifestyles following the warfare. There end up a robust reluctance to serve within the military, however others have been keen to accomplish that and did now not want to go back to the land. Conquest wars and extended durations of responsibility supplied a career, however one which have become insecure because of the absence of a everlasting fleet.

During the Republic, there has been no eternal fleet, however the truth that ships had been built and prepared as desired. The Roman fleet carried out a critical difficulty in her conquest of the Mediterranean globe, however it did no longer correctly manipulate the waters during peacetime, making piracy a huge chance to Italian transport. The wellknown vessel became the quinquereme, trireme, quadrireme, in addition to lighter ships just like the Illyrian lembi.

Business and Currency

Peasants in Rome have been flanked by way of using commercial agencies: the Etruscans and the Greek colonists. Etruria started out out energetic buying and selling with Greece within the seventh century, shipping Egyptian and Assyrian-fashion devices to Italy. An Etruscan school of painters emerged, inspired by using imported models. Corinthian merchandise ruled Etruscan markets within the seventh century, decided with the useful resource of Greek imports and impacts within the route of the following century. The sixth century witnessed the Greek colonization of Massilia, the improvement of Carthage, the alliance amongst Etruria and Carthage in the direction of the Greeks, the decline of Greek competition in the west, and Etruscan dominance in Latium. Many cities determined a boom in company, with temples and civic homes bobbing up. Early Rome grow to be commonly worried with agriculture and wars in preference to alternate. The departure of courtroom docket docket lifestyles brought about a less hard u . S . A ., with Etruscan luxurious losing way to more fundamental nearby usages.

Following the Gallic invasion, Rome, a Greek metropolis, rose to prominence inside the fourth century BC. The metropolis's partitions encompassed 1,060 acres, extra than instances that of Capua and five instances that of Ardea. Rome's growth into Greek-endorsed areas brought about pottery made on Attic fashions and a thriving bronze organisation. However, direct exposure to Greek paintings thru contacts with Etruria and Campania did now not elicit not unusual admiration. The Romans were disinterested in trade, and their % with Carthage famous the Carthaginians to extend their port and construct a modest fortification in Ostia.

The Roman conquest of Italy gave blessings to populace, appreciably commercium, however the conquest of the

Mediterranean unfold out new possibilities. The ruling elite did not are looking for new markets for Italian organization, who choose community management. The 0.33 century noticed little increase in Roman production, with conflicts with Carthage encouraging the manufacture of armaments and navy tool. Etruria's cities have emerge as an increasing number of rich, however creative idea diminished. In the second century, slave tough work changed free labor, and the small hold tool flourished. Although global alternate grew, it held little hobby for Roman aristocrats or have an effect on over politics. The developing call for for steeply-priced boosted change, but the aristocracy maintained its entrenched hobbies in land and difficult paintings.

Roman cash originated in southern Italy about 340 BC, at the same time as the arrival of Rome's early coinage came about later. Early values have been calculated in phrases of oxen and sheep, ensuing within the name pecunia (cash). In 289, the mint's trivir place of job have grow to be fashioned, and real coins, which encompass round bronze asses, have been minted. Due to the warfare with Pyrrhus and expanded conversation with southern Italy, Rome produced silver cash classified ROMANO (RUM) for navy use. The Hannibalic War had a great impact on coinage, with the weight of the ass reducing and the creation of a cutting-edge silver denarius. Roman forex took over, with the Romans claiming a monopoly after the Hannibalic War. The country's monetary pointers aligned with its political increase.

During the First Punic War and the Hannibalic War, the Roman treasury took on more duties, with the value expected at kind of one hundred million denarii. Taxation became the number one deliver of income, with the treasury following the model of a Greek 'liturgy' or a contemporary battle mortgage. The war rate the Roman treasury almost 3½ instances more every year than in the route of the First Punic warfare. National wealth grew fast in the early part of the second century, with Roman belongings values doubling or tripling by using manner of one hundred and fifty BC. War indemnities, loot, and Spanish mines provided extra belongings of sales. Money had little shopping for energy, with a bushel of wheat costing three denarii, olive oil costing 10 denarii, and farm slaves costing around 500 denarii.

Family Life in Rome

Rome's peasants have been flanked by means of manner of way of industrial corporation companies: Etruscans and Greek colonists. In the seventh century, Etruria resumed energetic exchange with Greece, bringing Egyptian and Assyrian-style merchandise to Italy. An Etruscan college of artists fashioned, drawing idea from imported fashions. Corinthian items ruled Etruscan markets inside the seventh century, and their effect changed into especially obvious in Etruscan paintings.

Etruria saw the doorway of Attic pottery inside the 6th century, and Greek imports and affects dominated for the subsequent century. Etruscan potters continued to make bucchero pottery, however Greek styles have turn out to be stylish. The sixth century witnessed the Greek colonization of Massilia, the boom of Carthage, the alliance of Etruria and Carthage in the direction of the Greeks, the fall of Greek competition in the west, the extension of Punic coverage, and the Etruscan supremacy of Latium.

Many cities observed massive commercial enterprise interest, together with Praeneste, which have grow to be an industrial powerhouse. Commerce moved through way from Etruria to Praeneste, at the equal time as Greek and Phoenician commodities arrived in Latium thru the port of Satricum. The temples at Velitrae, Ardea, and Satricum display the growth of enterprise and artwork in Latium.

Rome's reference to Italian organisation stays uncertain, but with the arrival of the Etruscans, the villages became citizens of a rich and powerful town. Industry grew with the inspiration of 8 difficult work guilds and control over the salt change. By the middle of the 5th century, Rome had reverted to a less difficult polity, with agriculture and the army taking precedence over company and exchange.

Following the Gallic invasion, Rome, a Greek city, got here to prominence inside the fourth century BCE. The advent of the 'Servian' walls took tremendous exertions and employed five million cubic ft of reduce stone. Rome's expansion into Greek-prompted territories produced Attic-fashion pottery, work of art in tombs at Paestum and Capua, and a booming bronze enterprise in the Latin colony of Cales.

In the second century, Romans from wealthy families delegated manufacturing to the lower training, however slave difficult paintings sooner or later supplanted loose tough work. The small preserve system remained, with livestock, fish, and vegetables provided in various marketplaces spherical Rome. Outside trade, in particular with the East, have become of little trouble to Roman elites or effect over Roman politics.

Roman coinage modified into designed to serve army rather than commercial enterprise capabilities, and the dominion's economic policy observed the sample of its political improvement. Following the Hannibalic War, Roman coinage grade by grade obtained dominance, and indigenous silver (argentum Oscense) modified into allowed to circulate in Spain. Carthage persevered to create cash, while Roman victories inside the East despatched monies yet again to Rome.

Chapter 10: The Foundation of Rome

1Mythical Origins: Romulus and Remus

One of the maximum well-known stories in ancient Roman mythology is that of Romulus and Remus, dual brothers who are said to be the founders of the metropolis of Rome. The legend of Romulus and Remus has turn out to be a massive a part of the legendary origins of Ancient Rome and it has even been depicted in numerous sorts of art work and literature over the centuries. However, beyond the fantastical elements of the story, there lies a deeper connection some of the legend and the upward thrust and fall of the Roman Empire.

The tale starts off evolved off evolved with the begin of dual brothers, Romulus and Remus, to the god Mars and the priestess Rhea Silvia. As babies, they had been abandoned through their mom and left to die within the Tiber River. However, the river god Tiberinus stored them and that they have been ultimately placed and raised with the resource of a she-wolf named Lupa. It is said that she fed and nurtured them till they were determined via a shepherd named Faustulus, who raised them as his private sons.

As they grew older, Romulus and Remus have end up expert hunters and that they've been also recognized to be fierce warriors. They decided to establish a town on the land in which they were raised through the she-wolf. However, they could not agree on the vicinity of the metropolis and a dispute arose between them. Romulus favored to assemble the metropolis on Palatine Hill, at the equal time as Remus desired it on Aventine Hill. In order to settle the dispute, they decided to are trying to find advice from the gods through augury, a form of divination the use of birds.

Remus found six vultures first, which he interpreted as a signal from the gods. However, hastily after, Romulus observed twelve vultures and claimed victory. In a match of anger, Remus mocked his brother's desire and in retaliation, Romulus killed him, consequently becoming the most effective ruler of the town. He named the town Rome after himself and declared it as the new middle of power within the vicinity.

The story of Romulus and Remus has a wealth of fantastical factors, along side gods, goddesses, and supernatural beings. However, it also holds a deeper which means in terms of the origins of Ancient Rome and its eventual upward thrust and fall.

One of the most vast elements of the legend is the idea of divine intervention. The story units the inspiration for the belief that the achievement of Rome have become a end end result of the choose of the gods. The involvement of gods and goddesses in the story symbolizes the religious ideals and practices of the historic Romans, which completed a critical position in the upward push of the Roman Empire.

The founding of Rome with the aid of way of Romulus also indicates the Roman values of electricity and electricity. The town emerge as installed through pressure and violence, and this technique of increase have become a defining function of the Roman Empire. The Romans have been appeared for his or her military prowess and their capacity to conquer and assimilate extremely good cultures into their very very personal.

Additionally, the rivalry amongst Romulus and Remus and their eventual separation mirrors the internal struggle for strength and manage in Rome, which performed a fantastic position in its downfall. The killing of Remus via his brother is a foreshadowing of the common civil wars and political assassinations that plagued the Roman Empire in its later years.

Moreover, the story of Romulus and Remus additionally sheds slight at the concept of management in Ancient Rome. Romulus modified into depicted as a sturdy and ambitious chief, willing to do a little element it takes to set up and keep his electricity. This shows the Roman perception within the importance of a sturdy and decisive leader, which modified into critical inside the growth and achievement of the empire.

On the opportunity hand, Remus, who modified into greater peaceful and diplomatic, represents the weaker and lots much less favored management fashion, which in the long run brought approximately his death. This highlights the Roman notion in the superiority of a sturdy and competitive leader, which may additionally have contributed to the downfall of the empire as properly.

Furthermore, the founding of Rome through Romulus and the following increase of the city additionally replicate the Roman ideology of development and improvement. Through strategic alliances and military conquests, the city of Rome multiplied swiftly, turning into a photograph of wealth, power, and civilization. However, this success moreover added about Rome's downfall, as its growth positioned a pressure on resources and brought approximately progressed inner conflicts.

The story of Romulus and Remus serves as a powerful picture of the mythical origins of Ancient Rome and its next upward thrust and fall. Beyond its fantastical elements, the legend holds a deeper which means in terms of the values, ideals, and ideologies of the ancient Romans, which common the route of their civilization. The tale of Romulus and Remus remains a large a part of Roman mythology and serves as a reminder of the enduring legacy of the Roman Empire.

2Historical Beginnings: The Seven Kings

Ancient Rome is a civilization that has captivated the imagination and interest of people for hundreds of years. From its humble beginnings as a small village at the banks of the Tiber River, Rome went at once to come to be one of the maximum powerful and influential empires inside the information of the arena. This upward push to greatness became in huge element attributed to the management of seven kings, who guided the town via severa worrying situations and mounted the inspiration for its eventual domination.

The history of historic Rome may be traced again to the 8th century BCE, while the city end up based with the aid of the mythical twins Romulus and Remus. According to legend, the twins have been raised by way of a she-wolf and went on to located the city at the Palatine Hill. This occasion is venerated in Roman mythology as the founding of the city and is celebrated every year on April twenty first as the competition of Parilia.

The first king of Rome modified into Romulus, who is stated to have dominated from 753 BCE to 715 BCE. Under his rule, Rome extended its territory and mounted itself as a primary strength inside the Italian peninsula. Romulus is also credited with the development of most of the Roman institutions, which incorporates the Senate and the Legions.

After the dying of Romulus, the throne changed into taken over through using Numa Pompilius, who was identified for his piety and facts. He dominated from 715 BCE to 673 BCE and is top notch remembered for his spiritual reforms and the reputation quo of the Roman calendar. Numa modified into furthermore answerable for the construction of numerous temples and shrines, which similarly solidified the religious element of Roman society.

The 1/three king, Tullus Hostilius, have become appeared for his navy conquests and expansionist policies. He ruled from 673 BCE to 642 BCE and beneath his reign, Rome annexed severa neighboring territories. Tullus is likewise remembered for his position in the struggle towards Alba Longa, a metropolis that changed into visible as a rival to Rome. This struggle resulted in the destruction of Alba Longa and the consolidation of Rome's strength within the region.

Ancus Marcius, the fourth king of Rome, have become stated for his absolutely and easy rule. He have become the grandson of Numa Pompilius and ruled from 642 BCE to 617 BCE. During his reign, Rome observed giant increase in alternate and exchange, which further strengthened its monetary power. Ancus is also credited with the improvement of the primary bridge over the Tiber River and the boom of the city's port, which allowed for less complicated get proper of entry to to the ocean.

The fifth king, Lucius Tarquinius Priscus, have become the number one Etruscan king of Rome. He dominated from 616 BCE to 578 BCE and is remembered for his bold creation tasks, on the facet of the Cloaca Maxima (a sewer machine) and the Circus Maximus (a common performance venue). He furthermore progressed the town's navy, installing the number one reliable status navy of Rome.

Upon Tarquinius Priscus' loss of lifestyles, his son-in-law Servius Tullius took over due to the fact the 6th king of Rome. He ruled from 578 BCE to 534 BCE and is taken into consideration to be one of the maximum successful and influential kings in Roman information. Servius is remembered for his social reforms, together with the reputation quo of the first census and the reform of the Roman army. He moreover constructed the Servian Wall, a shielding shape that later have become the concept for the town's well-known Aurelian Walls.

The 7th and very last king of Rome became Lucius Tarquinius Superbus, or Tarquin the Proud. He ruled from 534 BCE to 509 BCE and became regarded for his tyrannical rule, which in the long run delivered about his downfall. Tarquin's reign turned into marked through corruption, oppression, and violence, which in the long run sparked a rebellion and the stop of the Roman monarchy.

The overthrow of Tarquin and the subsequent popularity quo of the Roman Republic marked the give up of the monarchy and the start of a modern day generation in Roman records. However, the legacy of the seven kings and their contributions to the city's increase and improvement endured to shape and feature an impact on the Republic and later, the Roman Empire.

The length of the seven kings is a essential a part of historic Rome's facts, because it laid the inspiration for the city's upward push to energy and eventual domination of the Mediterranean global. The installation order of sturdy institutions, growth of territory, and army enhancements all performed a essential function in Rome's boom and fulfillment.

Furthermore, the reign of the seven kings highlighted the significance of manage and the effect it is able to have on a civilization. Each king, in their non-public manner, contributed to Rome's development and left an extended-lasting legacy that could shape the path of records for hundreds of years to return.

The seven kings of ancient Rome finished a important feature in the metropolis's rise to greatness. From Romulus' humble beginnings to the tyrannical rule of Tarquin the Proud, every king left a mark on the town and paved the way for its eventual dominance as one of the greatest empires inside the international. Their legacy lives on inside the enduring effect of Roman way of life, language, and institutions, reminding us of the enduring impact of these historic rulers.

3Formation of the Roman Republic

The Roman Republic is a duration in Ancient Rome's records characterized through using way of the upward thrust of a powerful, democratic authorities that ruled over the Italian Peninsula and a full-size territory beyond. This duration spanned for over 5 centuries, from 509 BC to 27 BC, and laid the foundation for the formation of the Roman Empire. The Republic modified right into a vital generation in Roman records, marked through massive political, social, and monetary adjustments that usual the inspiration of Western civilization.

The origins of the Roman Republic may be traced decrease again to the sixth century

BC, when Rome modified right right into a small city-country ruled via a monarchy. The Etruscans, a effective neighboring civilization, had set up a monarchy in Rome with the ruling families referred to as the Tarquins. However, in 509 BC, after years of tyrannical rule with the useful resource of the Tarquin kings, the Roman residents revolted and drove them out of the metropolis. This brought about the status quo of a new shape of government, a republic, in which energy come to be shared amongst governing our our bodies, the Senate and the Assembly.

The formation of the Republic have become a big turning factor for Rome because it marked the start of a democratic government, wherein the human beings had a say in the choice-making approach of the country. The Senate, which includes 3 hundred participants, turn out to be liable for providing and debating prison guidelines, dealing with foreign family people, and controlling public charge variety, at the same time as the Assembly, crafted from male citizens, had the strength to vote on criminal hints and pick magistrates. This gadget of tests and balances ensured that no character or employer had absolute strength, and selections had been made with the super interests of the Roman humans in mind.

The Roman Republic moreover noticed tremendous adjustments in terms of expansion and conquest. As Rome grew in energy and feature an impact on, it began out to increase its territory, grade by grade conquering the Italian Peninsula through a sequence of wars with neighboring tribes and town-states. This growth introduced wealth and belongings to Rome, leading to the upward push of a rich and powerful magnificence of Roman residents referred to as patricians. With their wealth and effect, the patricians dominated the government, main to a growing divide between them and the majority of Roman citizens, called plebeians. This divide have turn out to be a massive issue that would contribute to the eventual downfall of the Republic.

One of the defining events in the facts of the Roman Republic modified into the Punic Wars, a series of 3 wars fought amongst Rome and Carthage, a powerful Phoenician city-nation in North Africa. The first Punic War, fought from 264 BC to 241 BC, marked Rome's first number one distant places conquest and installation it as a dominant naval electricity in the Mediterranean. The 2d and zero.33 Punic Wars, fought in 218 BC and 149 BC, respectively, resulted in the eventual destruction of Carthage and the purchase of its territories with the aid of way of Rome. These wars not great prolonged Rome's territory however furthermore introduced in big quantities of wealth and assets, fueling the Republic's financial device and growth.

As Rome persisted to increase, it confronted several annoying situations, together with social and political unrest. The massive amount of wealth and territory brought with the resource of conquest brought on a widening hole a number of the patricians and the plebeians, predominant to not unusual conflicts a few of the 2 classes. The plebeians, who made up the bulk of the populace, demanded extra rights and illustration within the government, leading to the creation of tribunes, who've been elected representatives of the plebeians. The struggle between the patricians and plebeians for political power and illustration ought to keep inside the course of the Republic's records and be one of the contributing factors to its eventual fall.

The downfall of the Roman Republic commenced inside the second century BC at the same time as political corruption and developing monetary inequality ended in political instability and civil unrest. The upward push of powerful military leaders, referred to as generals, who had received reputation and loyalty thru military conquests and guarantees of land and rewards, additionally threatened the Republic's stability. One of the maximum well-known of those generals became Julius Caesar, who acquired manipulate of Rome thru navy strain and declared himself the dictator for lifestyles in 40 4 BC. His rule marked the cease of the Republic, and he become assassinated by way of using a group of senators who feared his developing energy.

The demise of Caesar sparked a series of civil wars that might ultimately result in the upward push of the Roman Empire. Caesar's nephew, Octavian, emerged powerful from those conflicts and modified into declared the number one emperor of Rome in 27 BC, marking the end of the Republic and the begin of the Roman Empire. The Republic's downfall may be attributed to various factors, together with political corruption, financial inequality, and societal divisions.

The formation of the Roman Republic done a important function inside the rise and fall of the Roman Empire. It marked a period of incredible expansion, political trade, and improvements in engineering, artwork, and literature that laid the inspiration for Western civilization. However, the Republic's downfall, marked with the resource of the usage of political instability, civil wars, and the rise of authoritarian leaders, introduced about the repute quo of an empire that could decline and fall in the fifth century AD. The legacy of the Roman Republic keeps to influence current political systems, making it a brilliant period in Ancient Rome's records.

Chapter 11: The Roman Republic

4Political Structure and Institutions

The Roman Republic is regularly visible because the start of the Roman Empire, which has had a profound effect on Western civilization. The Republic lasted for almost 500 years, from 509 BC to 27 BC, and in a few unspecified time within the destiny of this time, the Romans installed a robust political shape and institutions that paved the way for their eventual upward thrust and fall as an empire.

The political form of the Roman Republic turn out to be based totally totally on a well-defined device of presidency that changed into divided into 3 branches: the Consuls, the Senate, and the Assemblies. The Consuls had been the satisfactory elected officers within the Republic and served as co-rulers of Rome. They have been elected for a one-12 months time period and were answerable for overseeing the military, challenge remote places affairs, and presiding over the Senate and Assemblies.

The Senate emerge as an advisory frame made from 3 hundred wealthy and effective guys from the patrician magnificence. They were appointed for lifestyles and held big effect over the Republic's preference-making method. The Senate come to be accountable for imparting and debating criminal hints, supervising the Consuls, and handling Rome's budget and overseas affairs.

The Assemblies, however, were our our our bodies made from the commonplace people of Rome, called plebeians. The Assemblies consisted of three vital our bodies: the Comitia Centuriata, the Comitia Tributa, and the Concilium Plebis. These assemblies had the power to vote on criminal recommendations, declare conflict, and decide on officials which consist of the Tribunes, who represented the pursuits of the plebeians.

One of the important factor factors contributing to the success of the Roman Republic have become its robust crook and political establishments. The Romans superior an complicated prison device that come to be primarily based totally on the principle of identical protection beneath the regulation. This tool included written legal recommendations, trial techniques, and the idea of innocent until confirmed accountable. As a quit end result, Roman citizens enjoyed a feel of protection and fairness in their dealings with the government, which promoted balance and order inside the Republic.

Another vital detail of the Republic's political form turned into the concept of tests and balances. The Roman Republic turned into a mixed government, combining factors of monarchy, aristocracy, and democracy. This device ensured that no single branch of presidency held an excessive amount of energy, hence preventing the rise of a tyrant or dictator. The Consuls have to veto every unique's alternatives, the Senate should veto the Consuls, and the Tribunes should veto the Senate. This stability of electricity helped keep balance and avoided every body business enterprise from becoming too dominant.

With the growing boom of the Roman Republic, the want for inexperienced control and choice-making have come to be obvious. To deal with this, the Romans advanced a complicated system of provincial authorities. They set up provinces in conquered territories, which were ruled with the useful aid of appointed officers referred to as Proconsuls and Propraetors. These officers have been accountable for gathering taxes, maintaining order, and enforcing Roman law in their provinces.

The Roman Republic's political shape and institutions moreover accomplished a massive function inside the military's improvement. The Roman navy emerge as alternatively prepared and disciplined, and its fulfillment may be attributed to its hierarchical shape and strong experience of duty to the dominion. The Consuls served as commanders-in-chief of the navy, and the Senate changed into liable for appointing military leaders. As the Republic expanded, the Roman navy became a crucial tool in conquering new territories and keeping manipulate over conquered lands.

However, regardless of the strong political form and establishments inside the Roman Republic, it ultimately fell due to a aggregate of internal and external elements. The growing gap most of the wealthy and terrible, political corruption, and a weakening army all contributed to the Republic's decline. In addition, the developing reliance on slave labor and the depletion of sources brought on financial instability and a decline in political and social brotherly love.

The upward push of effective military generals, collectively with Julius Caesar, additionally contributed substantially to the Republic's downfall. These generals broke the stability of energy and used their navy may additionally to gain manipulate over the Roman authorities. In 27 BC, Caesar's observed son, Octavian, took control of the Roman government and hooked up the Roman Empire, marking the surrender of the Republic.

The political shape and institutions of the Roman Republic have been crucial to the upward push and fall of the Roman Empire. The Republic's properly-defined system of government, sturdy criminal and political establishments, and assessments and balances promoted balance and contributed to its achievement for nearly five centuries. However, through the years, internal and outdoor factors added approximately the Republic's decline and paved the way for the repute quo of the Roman Empire.

Nevertheless, the Republic's legacy maintains to influence contemporary political systems and institutions.

5 Expansion and Conquests

The Roman Republic, which lasted from 509 BCE to 27 BCE, modified right into a duration of boom and conquests that shaped the muse of the Roman Empire. This generation noticed the rise and fall of the Roman Republic, leaving an indelible mark at the route of history.

The growth of the Roman Republic end up driven with the aid of a combination of political, monetary, and military factors. Rome's vicinity on the center of the Mediterranean made it a strategic factor for trade and trade. This, in turn, delivered wealth and prosperity to the metropolis, thinking of the financing of ambitious navy campaigns. Additionally, the Roman Republic have become a exceptionally organized nation with a strong important government, green bureaucracy, and a powerful army. These factors gave Rome the political and army stability to extend its territory and assert its dominance over neighboring areas.

In the early years of the Republic, Rome's conquests were typically centered on the Italian peninsula. The Romans engaged in a sequence of wars with their neighboring town-states, known as the Latin War, which ultimately brought about Rome's victory and the mounted order of its first territorial earnings. These early victories paved the way for in addition enlargement, and via using the 3rd century BCE, Rome had prolonged its manage over most of essential and southern Italy.

The Roman Republic additionally stepped forward its territory through the use of alliances and international individuals of the family as opposed to actually relying on army strain. This have become confirmed with the appearance of the Latin League, a protecting alliance between Rome and the neighboring Latin cities. Through this alliance, Rome gained valuable navy and economic resource, which aided in its similarly conquests. The Roman Republic additionally fashioned alliances with different powers, together with the Kingdom of Syracuse in Sicily, allowing them to benefit manipulate of the island and installation it as their first province.

With the Italian peninsula in huge issue underneath their manipulate, the Romans started out to set their factors of interest on increasing beyond their borders. This caused the first Punic War (264-241 BCE), a series of conflicts towards the effective North African city of Carthage. The conflict modified into extensively speaking fought over manipulate of buying and selling routes and belongings within the Mediterranean. The Roman army, underneath the control of admiral Gaius Duilius, secured a decisive victory over Carthage at the Battle of Mylae, putting in Rome as a dominant naval strength.

Victory inside the Punic Wars marked a superb turning factor for the Roman Republic, as it obtained manage of territories out of doors the Italian peninsula. These territories, together with Sicily, Sardinia, Corsica, and additives of Spain, provided Rome with precious sources and stepped forward its monetary strength. However, this expansion moreover introduced about new demanding situations due to the reality the Roman Republic struggled to manipulate and combine these territories into its political device.

The Roman Republic persisted its enlargement through a sequence of conflicts and wars over the following century. The Second Punic War (218-201 BCE) observed Rome engage in a fierce battle with Carthage all all yet again, this time below the control of the army genius Hannibal. Despite initial setbacks, the

Romans have been in the end able to defeat the Carthaginian military and increase their territory into Spain and North Africa.

The Roman conquest of Greece in the Macedonian Wars (215-148 BCE) emerge as each different giant growth of the Republic. These wars had been fueled via manner of using opposition and electricity struggles amongst Rome and the Hellenistic kingdoms. The Romans emerged excellent, gaining control of Greece and putting in it as a province, which similarly extended their affect and electricity in the Mediterranean.

With every conquest, the Roman Republic grew in duration, wealth, and power, enticing inside the peak of its growth within the 1st century BCE. However, this era of increase and conquest moreover marked the start of the Republic's decline. As Rome persevered to expand, it confronted new stressful conditions, collectively with growing social and monetary inequalities, political corruption, and the stress of keeping a huge empire. These issues, mixed with the upward push of ambitious navy leaders, in the end introduced at the fall of the Republic.

One of the maximum well-known sports in Roman information and a turning point for the Republic turn out to be the assassination of Julius Caesar in 44 BCE. Caesar, a successful army elegant and famous baby-kisser, had extensively progressed Rome's territory at some point of his rule. His loss of life marked the surrender of the Republic and the start of the Roman Empire, as his adopted son Octavian emerged as the first emperor of Rome.

The expansion and conquests of the Roman Republic executed a crucial feature in shaping the upward push and fall of the Roman Empire. Through military may possibly, alliances, and strategic alliances, the Republic modified into able to expand its territory and assert its dominance within the Mediterranean region. However, this increase ultimately delivered approximately its downfall, due to the fact the demanding situations of governing this sort of high-quality empire proved to be too high-quality.

6Social and Economic Developments

The Roman Republic finished a critical position in shaping the ancient Roman Empire, which stays one of the most iconic and influential civilizations in information. This duration of records, spanning over 500 years, have come to be marked through large social and financial dispositions that finished a critical function in the upward push and fall of the Roman Empire.

Social Developments

During the Roman Republic, there were super social modifications that passed off inside the society. The Roman Republic have become to start with ruled with the aid of kings. However, in 509 BC, the Romans overthrew the monarchy and established a republican form of presidency. This shift in energy marked the begin of the Roman Republic, with a Senate and consuls because the valuable governing our our our bodies.

One of the most splendid social dispositions throughout this period became the growth of Roman citizenship. Initially, best patricians, the wealthy and influential elegance of residents, had the right to participate in politics and hold public administrative center. However, over the years, plebeians, the common people, have been granted citizenship and had been allowed to keep political positions. This circulate now not nice helped to solidify the strength of the Roman kingdom, but it moreover created a revel in of concord the numerous humans.

Another remarkable social development sooner or later of the Roman Republic have become the emergence of the elegance device. As the Roman financial gadget grew, social education have grow to be greater described. The higher magnificence protected rich traders, landowners, and individuals of the Roman aristocracy. The middle splendor consisted of professional humans and small industrial organization proprietors, at the same time as the lower elegance come to be made from slaves and terrible farmers. This class department had a big impact on the social and economic dynamics of the Roman Republic.

Economic Developments

The Roman Republic moreover witnessed large monetary tendencies that executed a essential characteristic in its upward push and fall. During this period, the Roman economic machine skilled fantastic increase and prosperity. The conquest of neighboring territories and the boom of trade routes contributed notably to the economic achievement of the Republic.

One of the maximum vital economic inclinations inside the direction of this period turn out to be the shift from an agriculture-based completely completely financial system to a extra marketplace-orientated one. As the Roman Republic grew, a marketplace for gadgets and offerings emerged, principal to the rise of a cash financial system. This shift not only contributed to the increase of the Roman monetary machine but also revolutionized trade and commerce within the Mediterranean location.

The dominance of Rome within the Mediterranean place additionally added approximately the fame quo of a massive community of alternate routes, connecting the Roman Republic to its conquered territories and past. This exchange network delivered approximately the spread of Roman goods, subculture, and ideas, in addition solidifying the empire's monetary electricity.

The boom of the economic device in a few unspecified time in the destiny of the Roman Republic additionally had a large effect at the social form. As wealth multiplied, the distance many of the rich and terrible widened, fundamental to social tensions. The wealthy elite, called the patricians, used their wealth to gain political electricity, on the identical time because the lower training struggled to make a dwelling. This disparity must in the long run reason social unrest and make contributions to the downfall of the Roman Republic.

The Rise and Fall of the Roman Empire

The social and economic traits during the Roman Republic in the long run performed a critical role inside the rise and fall of the Roman Empire. The increase of citizenship helped to assemble a sense of group spirit some of the people and facilitate the increase of the empire. However, because the empire persevered to amplify, the distance between the wealthy and terrible widened, important to social and financial instability.

The financial prosperity of the Roman Republic moreover delivered about immoderate spending and corruption the various ruling elite. This, coupled with unsustainable enlargement and army campaigns, introduced approximately monetary stress and financial crises, ultimately contributing to the fall of the Roman Empire.

The social and economic inclinations of the Roman Republic done a important characteristic in the upward thrust and fall of the Roman Empire. The expansion of citizenship, growth of the monetary device, and standing quo of exchange networks helped to build a powerful empire. However, the developing wealth gap and excessive spending in the end delivered about the collapse of the Roman Republic, marking the stop of an generation in ancient Rome records.

7The Punic Wars and the Rise of Rome

The Punic Wars, a chain of conflicts amongst Rome and Carthage, carried out a vital function in the rise of Rome as a dominant electricity within the historical world. These wars, fought amongst 264 BC and 146 BC, not best long-established the future of Rome but additionally had tremendous implications for the complete Mediterranean vicinity and past. Through their victory over Carthage within the final Punic War, the Romans secured their role due to the truth the rulers of the Mediterranean and laid the standards for their empire that could eventually span at some point of 3 continents. This essay will speak the Punic Wars and their impact on the upward push of Rome as a republic, similarly to their function within the eventual fall of the Roman Empire.

The first Punic War (264-241 BC) turn out to be fought over manipulate of Sicily, an island rich in belongings and strategically located inside the Mediterranean. The battle began out out as a minor dispute between the town of Messana in Sicily and Syracuse, but speedy escalated proper into a whole-scale conflict among Rome and Carthage. The Romans, with their superior land navy, have been able to gain the top hand within the early degrees of the conflict. However, they short observed out the want for a navy to assignment Carthage's dominance at sea. With the assist of a captured Carthaginian ship and the talent in their leader, Gaius Duilius, the Romans built their first fleet and won a decisive naval war at Mylae in 260 BC. This victory now not best gave the Romans manipulate of the seas but also boosted their self notion in their military abilities.

The 2nd Punic War (218-201 BC) is probable the most well-known and massive of the three wars. It began even as the Carthaginian preferred Hannibal released a marvel attack on Saguntum, a town allied with Rome. Hannibal then led his military, which includes war elephants, in the course of the Alps and into Italy, primary a campaign this is however studied by way of way of the usage of navy strategists these days. Despite numerous early victories through Hannibal, the Romans have been able to shield their territory with a chain of tactical maneuvers, which incorporates the famous Battle of Cannae. But it become the Roman sizeable Scipio Africanus who ultimately became the tide of the war. In 202 BC, he defeated Hannibal at the Battle of Zama, efficiently ending the conflict and establishing Rome due to the truth the dominant energy in the western Mediterranean.

The 1/three and final Punic War (149-146 BC) become a end give up result of developing tensions between Rome and Carthage, similarly to the preceding's desire to increase its control over the Mediterranean. After a failed upward thrust up thru the Carthaginians inside the direction of Roman rule, the Romans determined an possibility to spoil their prolonged-time rival as speedy as and for all. Despite fierce resistance from the Carthaginians, Rome modified into able to defeat and triumph over Carthage, bringing an give up to the Punic Wars.

The effect of the Punic Wars on the rise of Rome as a republic turn out to be big. The wars no longer only set up Rome due to the fact the dominant strength inside the Mediterranean however moreover contributed to the increase of its empire. The acquisition of territories such as Sicily, Sardinia, and Corsica in a few unspecified time inside the future of the wars provided Rome with valuable belongings and extended its wealth. The wars additionally introduced about improvements in military generation and techniques, making Rome's navy one of the maximum feared within the historical worldwide. This helped the republic to further make bigger its territories through conquest and solidify its manage over the Mediterranean.

The Punic Wars moreover had a ways-attaining results for different civilizations in the Mediterranean place. The defeat of Carthage, a first-rate searching for and selling and naval electricity, via Rome had a widespread effect at the stableness of energy in the place. As Carthage emerge as compelled to cede its territories and pay reparations, the Romans have grow to be the undisputed rulers of the Mediterranean, paving the manner for the growth of their empire.

However, the upward thrust of Rome's empire moreover sowed the seeds of its eventual downfall. The Punic Wars, at the equal time as bringing wealth and energy to Rome, additionally created new social and economic issues in the republic. The influx of wealth from conquered territories caused a developing wealth-hole, with the aristocracy turning into increasingly more wealthy and corrupt while the not unusual humans suffered. This, alongside facet the non-forestall growth of the empire, located a strain on Rome's assets and resulted in monetary instability.

Furthermore, the ordinary struggle and growth additionally had a unfavorable impact on Rome's political device. The wars necessitated the growth of the Roman army, which required greater soldiers and sources. This caused the upward thrust of powerful military generals who frequently placed their very very own objectives above the pastimes of the republic, resulting in political instability and the eventual breakdown of the republican system of government.

The Punic Wars have been a pivotal occasion within the information of historic Rome, shaping the republic's rise to energy and laying the idea for its eventual downfall. Through those wars, Rome installation itself due to the truth the dominant pressure within the Mediterranean and acquired large wealth and assets. However, the wars moreover added about social, financial, and political problems that in the end contributed to the decline of the republic and the upward push of the Roman Empire.

Chapter 12: The Julius Caesar Era

Caesar's Military Campaigns

The call Julius Caesar is synonymous with strength, conquest, and management in Ancient Rome. He emerges as a renowned military strategist and flesh presser who accomplished a critical role within the upward thrust and fall of the Roman Empire. During his reign in the first century BC, Caesar's navy campaigns substantially extended the territory of Rome, in the long run important to the peak of its strength and have an impact on. However, those identical campaigns additionally sowed the seeds of its downfall. In this essay, we can explore Caesar's military campaigns, their significance in Ancient Rome's data, and their closing effect on the upward thrust and fall of the Roman Empire.

Caesar's rise to energy commenced whilst he modified into appointed due to the fact the governor of the Roman province of Gaul (modern-day-day France) in fifty 8 BC. This have emerge as a important 2d in Caesar's profession, as it allowed him to construct a sturdy and constant military, which could play a pivotal position in his future campaigns. The conquest of Gaul emerge as Caesar's best military success and the first of several successful campaigns that could cement his fame as a powerful leader.

Caesar's conquest of Gaul became no longer a easy trip; it involved numerous military campaigns that stretched over eight years. The first advertising campaign in fifty eight BC have end up closer to the Helvetii, a Gallic tribe, who've been making plans to migrate to the Roman province of Narbonensis. Caesar's victory in this advertising marketing campaign helped him installation dominance over the Gallic tribes and sturdy the southern border of the Roman Empire.

In fifty seven BC, Caesar launched right into a 2d marketing campaign in opposition to the Belgae, a confederation of tribes located in northern Gaul. This became a greater tough advertising and marketing campaign, with fierce resistance from the Belgae. However, Caesar's strategic maneuvers and superior army techniques triggered their eventual defeat, expanding Roman manage over the entire Gallic territory.

The following year, Caesar confronted a massive rebellion in the north of Gaul, led through the usage of the usage of the chieftain Vercingetorix. This marketing and advertising and marketing advertising and marketing campaign, known as the Gallic Wars, have become taken into consideration considered one of Caesar's maximum crucial navy campaigns, and it lasted for almost 3 years. It grow to be a fierce and brutal conflict, with each components committing atrocities. However, Caesar's management and tactical brilliance all yet again triumphed, and the Gallic tribes ultimately surrendered. With the defeat of Gaul, Caesar's military prowess and reputation spread throughout the Roman Empire, solidifying his feature as one in every of Rome's first-rate generals.

Caesar's subjugation of Gaul no longer simplest extended Roman territory but additionally brought first rate wealth to the empire. The conquest of Gaul supplied Rome with large reserves of gold, silver, and slaves, similarly to securing a critical alternate direction to the Atlantic. This newfound wealth allowed Caesar to enhance his political strength, as he used it to fund his lavish way of life and advantage beneficial resource from influential Roman elites.

After consolidating his manage over Gaul, Caesar set his attractions on conquering Britain. In fifty five BC, he launched a advertising and marketing marketing campaign to invade Britain, believing that it would be an easy victory. However, he faced fierce resistance from the nearby tribes, similarly to harsh weather conditions.

The marketing marketing campaign proved to be a failure, forcing Caesar to retreat and skip again to Gaul.

Caesar's navy campaigns in Gaul and Britain marked the pinnacle of his electricity and have an impact on in Rome. By increasing Roman territory and wealth, he received widespread popularity some of the commonplace people, making him an great stress in Rome's political panorama. However, this moreover sparked jealousy and worry amongst his fellow Roman leaders. To maintain his energy, Caesar had to strong a political function that could shield him from his enemies.

In forty nine BC, Caesar's political rival, Pompey, convinced the Roman Senate to reserve Caesar to disband his navy and pass back to Rome as a non-public citizen. Fearing prosecution, Caesar decided on to defy the Senate and lead his army at a few stage inside the Rubicon River, marking the begin of a civil warfare. Over the route of four years, Caesar's military engaged in numerous battles, together with the well-known Battle of Pharsalus, which in the long run precipitated his victory and solidification of his strength in Rome.

With his function due to the fact the undisputed leader of Rome, Caesar have come to be unfastened to put in force sweeping political reforms and hold his military conquests. He launched a marketing campaign against the ultimate final Roman Republic stronghold inside the Mediterranean area, the kingdom of Pontus, reigning a hit within the Battle of Zela in 47 BC. This event signified the transition from the Roman Republic to the Roman Empire.

However, regardless of his navy achievements and political energy, Caesar's arguable moves, along with maintaining himself dictator for life, made him a purpose of assassination. In 44 BC, a set of senators led through Marcus Junius Brutus and Gaius Cassius plotted and efficaciously assassinated Caesar, marking the prevent of the Julius Caesar technology.

The lack of life of Caesar introduced approximately a extended duration of turmoil and instability within the Roman Empire. The energy vacuum created with the aid of his dying became rapid filled with the useful resource of way of some other army standard, Caesar's notable-nephew, Octavian. Octavian, who later have grow to be called Augustus, consolidated energy and have grow to be Rome's first emperor, ushering in the golden age of the Roman Empire.